D0896558

ASSATA SHAKUR

A 20th Century Escaped Slave

By
Barbara Casey

Published in the United States of America by:

Strategic Media Books, Inc.
782 Wofford St., Rock Hill, SC 29730.
www.strategicmediabooks.com

Manufactured in the United States of America.

ISBN-10: 193-9521602
ISBN-13: 978-1939521606

Requests for permission should be directed to:
strategicmediabooks@gmail.com

or mailed to:

Permissions
Strategic Media Books, Inc.
782 Wofford St.
Rock Hill, SC 29730

Distributed to the trade by:

Cardinal Publishers Group
2402 North Shadeland Ave., Suite A
Indianapolis, IN 46219

DISCLAIMERS

The information presented in this book is based on federal and state court records and files, FBI memoranda and documents, secret service files, police records, and information in the media. All reasonable efforts have been made to credit sources and present the facts truthfully and coherently.

***

All of the quotations in this book are written as they appeared in the original source. No attempt has been made to correct spelling or punctuation.

AUTHOR'S NOTE

I wish to thank Alfredo Ferraro, professional translator and interpreter, for his assistance in translating into English from Spanish and Cuban Spanish, a form of Caribbean Spanish, West African, French, and indigenous Taino, the comments of Cuban bloggers on *www.14ymedio.com*.

OTHER BOOKS BY BARBARA CASEY

Nonfiction

Kathryn Kelly: The Moll behind Machine Gun Kelly

Fiction

The Gospel According to Prissy

The Cadence of Gypsies (Book 1 of The F.I.G. Mysteries)

The Wish Rider (Book 2 of The F.I.G. Mysteries)

The Clock Flower (Book 3 of The F.I.G. Mysteries)

The House of Kane

The Coach's Wife

Shyla's Initiative

Just Like Family

DEDICATION

For RC

For encouraging me to investigate

the joys of writing nonfiction.

Table of Contents

My name is Assata Shakur, and I am a 20th century escaped slave. Because of government persecution, I was left with no other choice than to flee from the political repression, racism and violence that dominate the U.S. government's policy towards people of color. I am an ex-political prisoner, and I have been living in exile in Cuba since 1984....

Assata Shakur

Chapter One

THE FORMATIVE YEARS

On May 2, 1973, around 12:45 a.m., Assata Shakur (born JoAnne Deborah Bryon), the godmother and step-aunt of slain rap star Tupac Shakur, along with Zayd Malik Shakur (born James F. Costan) and Sundiata Acoli (born Clark Squire), were stopped on the New Jersey Turnpike in East Brunswick by State Trooper James Harper for driving with a broken tail light and, according to Col. David B. Kelly of the New Jersey State Police, the vehicle was also "slightly" exceeding the speed limit. After calling the dispatcher and reporting his plans to stop the vehicle he had been following, Harper can later be heard to say: "Hold on— two black males, one female." The stop occurred 200 yards south of what was then the Turnpike Authority administration building at exit 9, the headquarters of Troop D. Trooper Werner Foerster arrived as backup a few minutes later in a second patrol vehicle (Car 820).

Zayd Shakur was driving the two-door vehicle, Assata Shakur (not related) was seated in the right front seat, and Sundiata Acoli was in the right rear seat. Trooper Harper asked the driver for his identification and vehicle registration, noticed a discrepancy, asked him to get out of the car, and began to question him at the rear of the vehicle. It was at this point, with the questioning of Zayd Shakur, that a confrontation occurred. In the ensuing shootout, Trooper Foerster was killed, shot four times, twice by a .38 caliber semiautomatic pistol and twice in the head with his own gun, execution style. Zayd Shakur was also killed, and Assata Shakur and Trooper Harper were wounded.

So begins the story of Assata Shakur and how, now 43 years later at the age of 69, she has come to define herself as a 20th century escaped slave.

***

Born in Queens, New York, and named JoAnne Deborah Bryon, Assata Shakur's father was an accountant for the federal government, and her mother, Doris Johnson, was an elementary school teacher. Assata spent her early childhood in the Bricktown section of Jamaica, New York, and, along with her mother who divorced shortly after her daughter's birth, was taken care of by her grandparents, Lulu and Frank Hill. Her maternal aunt, Evelyn Williams, was also involved in Assata's life from an early age, and made it a point to take her young niece under her wing as she got older – "exposing her to the nicer things" – by visiting museums, attending plays and movies, eating at various restaurants, and attending different churches.

Assata's birth records have never been found and, therefore, the actual date of when she entered this world is unsubstantiated. According to the FBI, Shakur has used August 19, 1952, as a birthdate at various times. However, the date of July 16, 1947, is what was printed on the FBI Wanted posters, and, therefore, is the date most often used. She had one sister who was five years younger named Beverly.

In 1950, when Assata was three years old, the family moved to a big wooden house on Seventh Street in Wilmington, North Carolina, where her grandfather had grown up as one of eleven children. Although many siblings and other relatives had moved away, there were a number of aunts and uncles and cousins still living in the area. One of Assata's favorite relatives on her grandfather's side was her Aunt Lou, a sister of Assata's great grandmother, Mama Jessie. Assata writes in her autobiography:

Aunt Lou had a magic house, full of all kinds of flavors, textures, smells, and things. There were whole worlds in her house to explore. She would always feed me something good to eat and then let me run wild.

Aunt Lou had a son, Willie, who apparently made a name for himself by tearing down the "colored" and "white only" signs wherever he found them, and breaking the Jim Crow laws as often as he could get away with it.

Assata's relatives on her grandmother's side lived in the town of Seabreeze, close to Carolina Beach just outside of Wilmington. Their name was Freeman, and they mostly worked as farmers and fishermen, and they ran their own small stores. Her maternal great grandfather and great grandmother, Alexander and Charity Freeman, who were of mixed African and Cherokee Indian heritage, and a part of the currently named Waccamaw-Siouan and Lumbee Tribes, owned a large parcel of land that bordered on the Cape Fear River and the Atlantic Ocean. A "free person of color," Alexander bought the former Sedgeley Abbey plantation from a white man in 1855. The house itself, believed to have been built during the Revolutionary War, was either in complete disrepair or already torn down, but the purchase included a 400-acre tract of land, some of which was cleared for growing indigo, corn, and cotton, and about 16 acres of swamp land that could be used for growing rice. With the land purchase, there was an adjoining 300-acre beach tract near Myrtle Grove Sound in the Federal Point Township.

In 1876, Alexander's descendant, Robert Bruce Freeman Sr., bought an additional 2500 acres for $1 an acre. At his death, Robert Freeman parceled the land in tracts, designed to be self-supporting waterfront properties, to his eleven children. Two of Robert Bruce Freeman's heirs, Rowland Freeman (sometimes known as "Rowlie" or "Rollie") and Nathan Freeman, would play the biggest role in developing Freeman Beach/Seabreeze into a resort between the 1920s and the 1960s as blacks from across eastern and central North Carolina, South Carolina, and Georgia and as far away as New York traveled to experience the white sandy beach and the growing entertainment/commercial area nearby. Many of the visitors had never seen the ocean before. Over the years, the beach community became home not only to generations of the Freemans, but to a number of other African American families as well.

It was during this time, when the South was completely segregated, that Assata's grandfather opened a business on their beach-front property for blacks that included a restaurant, lockers and showers where people could change their clothes, and an area with a jukebox and hard wood floors for dancing. It was named Freeman's Beach, although the locals called it Bop City, and it was that name which became known up and down the eastern seaboard coast.

Bop City was one of two North Carolina beaches available to African Americans during the Jim Crow era. The other was called Shell Island, just across Queens Inlet from Wrightsville, built by a multiracial group of Wilmington professionals. However, it was completely destroyed by fire after being open only three years. Freeman's Beach, "the resort of last resorts," was a little farther away, about 12 miles south of downtown near Carolina Beach, and more difficult to get to; but with Shell Island no longer available, it was the only other nonwhite beach option.

The first resort in Seabreeze was built in 1922. Two years later, a new 25-room hotel that included a dance hall was built by Madam Victoria Lofton on the Freeman land that extended from the river to the sound. Simpson's Hotel followed in 1925, and the Monte Carlo by the Sea built by Frank and Lulu Hill, Assata's grandparents, was thriving by the 1930s and 1940s.

The Wilmington Bus Company received a franchise granted by the North Carolina Utilities Commission on May 23, 1925, to operate a bus line from Wilmington to Seabreeze, thereby making Bop City more accessible to visitors. Soon, a number of other resort-related businesses—including bathhouses and music clubs known as "jump joints"—became part of the neighborhood, many of them owned and operated by members of the expanding Freeman clan. Prominent families such as the Spauldings of Durham—who made their fortune in the N.C. Mutual Insurance Co., among other things— also bought and developed resort properties at Seabreeze. Restaurants such as Barbecue Sam's, who kept a pig pen in the back yard to supply an open pit, and Mom's Kitchen did a thriving business. In addition to barbecue on a bun, crab cakes and clam fritters were the house specialties. Nearby, Daley's Pier and Restaurant was a popular spot for fishing and crabbing. And a candy store was run by a full-blooded American Indian known as Snakeman, who also operated a small circus with a Ferris wheel, hobby horses, chair planes, and a carousel.

By the 1940s, thousands of black GIs were flocking to Seabreeze from nearby bases and Bop City became known as a music mecca. Usually staying for the summer, musicians such as Jimmy Cavallo and the House Rockers performed songs like "Drinkin' Wine Spo Dee O De" and "Good Rockn' Tonight"; and Bobby "Blue" Bland sang his unique, story-telling songs that mixed gospel with rhythm and blues (R&B). "I just sing what I feel," he once explained when asked about his music. "It's about life. You get hurt, you get happy."

Music at Seabreeze was a bit different from Wrightsville and Carolina Beach because it was black swing and rhythm and blues— dance moves seemed suggestive and the volume was cranked up to an ear-splitting level that could be heard for miles around. Many historians give it credit for starting the beach shag, a six-step, eight-count dance pattern, that later became so popular a few miles down the road at Myrtle Beach, South Carolina.

This was a happy time for young Assata, and she spent many of her days and nights at the beach with her cousins, building forts or castles in the sand dunes, playing hide-and-seek, hunting for sea shells, or just sitting in her grandfather's old blue jeep, pretending to serve tea to paper dolls or daydreaming, "wool gathering" as some would say. That was also when she developed a love for reading, and every other week her grandfather visited the "colored" library on Red Cross Street to pick up ten or twelve books for her to read. She especially enjoyed reading about pirates and the Bobbsey twins.

The other thing that Assata loved as a young child was music, and she would often dance to the jukebox tunes of Fats Domino, Nat King Cole, Chuck Berry, Little Richard, the Platters, Dinah Washington, and Big Maybelle, among others, occasionally collecting tips—usually around 50 cents—for her spirited efforts.

While under their care, Assata's grandparents tried to instill in their young granddaughter a sense of dignity. "You're as good as anyone else. Don't let anybody tell you that they're better than you," her grandmother would tell her sternly. "Don't you let me hear about anybody walking over my grandbaby." Not surprising, these were the same lessons instilled in the minds of Assata's mother and her mother's younger sister, Evelyn.

For Assata's grandparents, pride and dignity were connected to position and money, and that meant having a nice house, nice clothes, and a nice car—things white people had. "That's why you've got to get your education so that you can be somebody and have something in life," they told Assata. Young Assata was also lectured on how she should play with "decent children" who came from "decent families" and not "alley rats," although the difference, Assata would later confess, she couldn't distinguish.

The importance of work was another lesson Assata's grandparents taught her. Every day she was expected to help in the restaurant, wiping down tables, putting bags of potato chips in the racks, and sodas in the cooler to be chilled. On occasion, she was given the responsibility of collecting the 50 cents required of visitors wishing to park in the large lot her grandfather had constructed on his property.

Not everyone who visited Freeman Beach, however, was there to enjoy the restaurants or the white sandy beach and the ocean beyond. Occasionally, people who disapproved of there being a "colored" business so close to Wilmington and Carolina Beach would try to frighten the black owners by destroying the parking lot and firing guns into the air.

In 1952, the opening of the artificial Carolina Beach Inlet caused irreparable beach erosion at Seabreeze. Two years later, on October 15, 1954, Hurricane Hazel made landfall, a category four storm with wind gusts reported in excess of 130 mph. It struck during high tide of a full moon creating storm surges of catastrophic proportions, completely wiping out Seabreeze, Carolina Beach and Kure Beach. Hurricane Connie followed a year later.

None of the property owners had flood insurance and federal aid wasn't available to them. Nevertheless, the Hills salvaged building materials from what had been destroyed, and by the following summer they had rebuilt the place with their own hands and reopened it for business. Then came Hurricane Diane in 1955, Helen in 1958, Donna in 1960 and Alma in 1962. By the end of the 1960s when desegregation opened other beaches to African Americans, Freeman Beach had lost its summer visitors.

***

Assata first attended school at the age of four where Mrs. Perkins taught her the fundamentals of reading, writing, and arithmetic in a small, two-room school on Red Cross Street in Wilmington. She then moved back to New York with her mother where she attended most of the first grade before returning to Wilmington to complete the first grade and the second at Gregory Elementary School. In her autobiography, Assata describes the school:

There was a big dirt yard next to the school where we would play and fight. We grew up fighting; it was really hard to get through school without a few fights, just to survive. But I always wondered what made people fight .... I used to look out on the remains of the sunken ship that tilted up in front of our beach and wonder how people had died in it. It was covered with green moss and I imagined skeletons floating around inside. The ship had been sunk during the

Civil War and I always wondered if it carried Northerners or Southerners. Back in those days I used to think the Northerners were the good guys.

Fearful that their granddaughter's education in the segregated North Carolina school system was inferior, the Freemans sent Assata back to New York to be with her mother who had remarried and was living in a middle-class, heavily Jewish, virtually all-white area of Queens. For the next several years, Assata attended school in Queens where she was often the only black child in her class. She thought of herself as a "child version of a goodwill ambassador out to prove that black people were not stupid or dirty or smelly or uncultured." She writes:

I carried out this mission as best I could to show that I was as good as they were. I never questioned the things they thought were good. White people said classical music was the highest form of music; white people said that ballet was the highest form of dance; and I accepted those things as true .... And everything they wanted, I wanted. If they wanted a Revlon doll, I wanted a Revlon doll. If they wanted a poodle jacket, I wanted a poodle jacket. If they wanted a Star of David necklace, I wanted a Star of David necklace. If they could act snobby, then I could act snobby. I saved my culture, my music, my dancing, the richness of black speech for the times when I was with my own people.

During the summers, Assata would return to Wilmington with her family, and help her grandparents at their restaurant. With each passing year, however, the differences between the black and white, the poor and rich, became more pronounced. As Assata reached her pre-pubescence years, the difficulties she faced were more challenging and complex. She had little understanding of world events other than the struggles that black people faced. News about Montgomery, Alabama, Martin Luther King, Jr., Rosa Parks, and Little Rock was what impacted her the most as she approached her critical teenage years.

The older she got, the more she grew into herself. Her mother and her stepfather were having problems and argued constantly, mostly about money, creating an environment where Assata didn't want to be. Even having gone to college and working as a teacher, Assata's mother didn't earn that much; and her stepfather, an employee of the post office, was paid a meager salary. She escaped by sitting in front of the television watching her favorite programs such as "Ozzie and Harriet," "Leave It to Beaver," and "Father Knows Best," going to movies, or riding buses and subways and exploring new neighborhoods: white, black, Puerto Rican, Chinatown, Little Italy—it didn't matter. More and more she stayed away from home for longer periods of time, sometimes not returning at all and depending on strangers to give her a place to stay.

When her mother and stepfather broke up, her mother took Assata and her younger sister to live in a housing complex in South Jamaica near New York Boulevard and Foch. For a while, Assata was content; but after a particularly bad argument with her mother, she moved out and went straight to Greenwich Village, thinking that was where she would fit in.

The many dangers Assata faced by living on the streets in the Village, especially being so young, were a constant threat. After several failed attempts, mostly illegal and involving various scams, to work in order to take care of herself, she found a place to live and, after buying makeup to use so she would look older, she landed a job as a waitress and barmaid hustling drinks at a place called Tony's on 3rd Street. Even so, with little experience or knowledge of the ways of the world, she wasn't prepared for the difficulties she would face living on her own. When a friend of her Aunt Evelyn spotted her one day on the street, she immediately called Assata's aunt to tell her where she was. Assata, only thirteen years old at the time, was more than relieved to go back with her Aunt Evelyn, her mother's sister.

***

Born in North Carolina, Evelyn Williams was one of two daughters of an automobile mechanic and a seamstress. After graduating with honors from Jamaica High School, she enrolled in Brooklyn College. She then went on to study law from St. John's University Law School in the late 1950s. While attending law school,

17

determined to become a trial lawyer with her own private practice, she also worked as a social worker, which she would remember in her autobiography as offering little satisfaction: "… the delinquents and their families, the surrounding community that had brought them to her, all poor and all defeated by the mere process of existing in a society that had failed to touch their lives except with rejecting hands—made it impossible for me to feel any gratification from the small results I was able to achieve."

It was through her work that she became involved in a high-profile case involving the children of Ethel and Julius Rosenberg, two American Communists executed in 1953 for espionage. The parties involved were the New York City Department of Welfare, the young boys' paternal grandmother, and a married couple—Anne and Able Meeropols—with whom the boys were then living. At the request of the New York State Supreme Court, Williams investigated the parties, made extensive visits to the boys, and battled the political maneuvering of the court system to come to a decision that was in the best interest of the already-traumatized children.

The Meeropols, who were not friends of the Rosenbergs but were members of the American Communist Party, had come into the boys' lives after a period of constant upheaval. From the time of their parents' arrests, and even after the execution, the brothers were passed from one home to another—first one grandmother looked after them, then another, then friends. For a brief spell, they were even sent to a shelter. The paranoia of the McCarthy era was such that many people—even family members—were terrified of being connected with the Rosenberg children, and many people who might have cared for them were too afraid to do so. Eventually, partly through the efforts of Evelyn Williams, the lyricist, librettist, and musician Abel Meeropol and his wife Anne, whose first two children had been stillborn, were allowed to adopt the two young boys, ages 6 and 10.

When Williams earned her Juris Doctor degree, she was one of two African Americans in a class of 154. Much of her work focused on service to the community, especially in the early years: New York City Department of Welfare, social investigator; New

York City Children's Court, probation officer; Harlem Youth Opportunities Unlimited; defense attorney for family real estate claims in North Carolina; New York University Law School, and supervisor of graduate Volunteers in Service to America (VISTA) program. It was later that she would become defense attorney for members of the Black Liberation Army.

Williams was admitted to the New York State bar in 1959 and began practicing criminal law, hoping to defend the poor, the uneducated, and the oppressed who could not otherwise afford legal representation. She set up an office with another female African American attorney and hired a male secretary. It was during this period that her older sister's troubled teenage daughter, "Joey," came to live with her.

Described by her aunt as "an artistically gifted, intelligent and questioning teenager who had chafed at authority from an early age," Assata moved in with her Aunt Evelyn who lived in a Brownstone garden apartment on 80th Street between Amsterdam and Columbus in Manhattan. There was one large room for sleeping, eating, and living, and it had a small kitchen and bathroom where the toilet was bolted onto a platform with an overhead tank and a chain to pull in order to flush it. The "garden" just outside was where their neighbors threw their garbage. And even though Evelyn tried to keep things neat and clean, the apartment was too small for two people, especially when Assata didn't care about keeping things picked up and orderly. This lack of attention or interest in keeping things "neat" and "clean" around her would later become a major source of disagreement with her husband, ultimately leading to divorce.

The area where they lived was exciting for Assata as she once again explored the nearby neighborhoods. Central Park and Riverside Park were both within easy walking distance, and the Museum of Natural History and the Metropolitan Museum of Art were close by as well, along with several other art galleries, all of which Assata visited often.

Originally settled primarily by Germans, the neighborhood where they lived was now occupied mostly by Puerto Ricans. Only a few of the apartments had been renovated, however, while most of the others, usually only one room, were run down and used by three, four, five or more people.

Finances were limited, as most of Williams' clients were black and poor. Even so, she was determined that "Joey" would complete her education and graduate. Assata was attending Junior High School 44, a public school, at the time; but Evelyn strongly encouraged her to take the entrance exam in order to attend Cathedral High School, a school known for its strong academic program and its strict dress code requiring uniforms. Assata passed the exam and began the ninth grade at her new school.

Assata usually spent her weekends with her mother or visiting one of her girlfriends, spending hours talking about Mississippi civil rights activist Medgar Evers, sit-ins, and freedom riders, or writing poetry about love and black people, or sometimes about hate and death. And every summer, she went with her family down South to visit her grandparents. They still had a business on the beach, but hurricanes had destroyed two of their buildings, including the restaurant. They opened another restaurant, this time on Red Cross Street. A local artist painted a seascape mural on the walls, and Assata worked there whenever she was visiting.

When the NAACP rented a building down just a few doors from the restaurant, it created a new source of interest for Assata. Sometimes she would stand outside the door and listen to the people talking about "integrating the South by sitting in, praying in, singing in, and about nonviolence." Integration was what she wanted because she had experienced the degrading, dehumanizing side of segregation in the South as it compared to what she experienced by living in the North and attending school there. A few years later she would change her mind, believing that blacks were equally dehumanized in the North as well.

Assata continued to live with her Aunt Evelyn while she attended high school, and visiting her mother on the weekends. Before graduating, however, at the age of 16 she decided to drop out of school, get a job, and once again try living on her own. Without a diploma, and little else going for her, Assata was hired for only the most menial and low-paying jobs. She recalls that unhappy time in her life in her autobiography:

It seemed that the whole world was made up of things I couldn't afford. After I paid the rent on my furnished room, spent carfare, and bought food, I had just enough money to buy an air sandwich .... My life was being spent pushing around meaningless papers that had nothing to do with living. I wasn't doing anything positive. I wasn't making anything, creating anything, or contributing to anything.

At Evelyn's insistence, Assata attended night school in order to get her GED, but that only created more impatience, frustration, and anger, always just barely under the surface, as Assata was fired from one job to the next, never settling down. After months of trying to succeed on her own and failing, she decided to move back in with her mother, now living in an apartment in Flushing, Queens, and enroll in Manhattan Community College, a two-year business and liberal arts college within the City University of New York (CUNY) system, in order to major in business administration with a focus on marketing or advertising. Once on campus, however, she changed her mind and signed up for only one business course; and the rest of the time she studied history, psychology, and sociology, and the school's expanding black studies program. She also was drawn to the activities of the student body.

૦ઙ ૪૦

21

Chapter Two

THE RADICALIZATION OF ASSATA SHAKUR

A period of social change and unrest dominated the 1960s. It was at this time that struggle and activity were exploding in the black consciousness, and nationalism was on the upswing. Color television displayed images of jungle combat in Vietnam and maimed soldiers returning home, protesters and priests destroying draft cards and American flags, and young passionate women burning their bras. Idealism transcended generations and permeated almost all levels of public life. Students on campuses across America, from Berkeley to New York, demanded desegregation and unrestricted free speech, believing idealistically that they were creating a new, and better, America. Conventional lifestyles, authority, and institutions at all levels were being challenged, as was the materialism, consumerism, and mania for success that drove American society. People explored alternative patterns of work and domesticity and condemned the traditions surrounding sex and marriage by simply ignoring them or replacing them with "free love." And they argued that all paths to deeper fulfillment, even those involving illicit drugs, could be justified in order to "find one's self" and wanting just to "be." Perhaps no period in American history has been filled with so much unrest experimentation, and such an expansive sense of possibilities.

In the spring and summer months of 1964, 1965, 1966, 1967 and 1968, massive black rebellions swept across almost every major U.S. city in the Northeast, Midwest and California. Presidents Lyndon Johnson and Richard Nixon, and many others, feared violent revolution and denounced the protesters. Only a few years earlier, President John Kennedy had stated in his address marking the first anniversary of the Alliance for Progress: "Those who make peaceful revolution impossible will make violent revolution inevitable."

Manhattan Community College had a high percentage of black and Third World students, and Assata joined a black organization on campus, the Society of Golden Drums, which was pushing for more courses in black studies, black teachers, cultural awareness, and programs more responsive to the needs of black students. In addition, Assata attended civil rights meetings and took part in impassioned discussions, and joined the political activities, protests, and sit-ins on campus and elsewhere. She also became a student-teacher during the summer teaching arts and crafts and assisting students who had difficulties in remedial reading and math programs.

Assata's perspective on history and current affairs, as well as her own self-image, was changing. She cut off her "conk" hairstyle and let it grow naturally into an Afro, and she changed her dress to reflect her African roots, letting that be a statement of who she was. She read everything she could to learn about politics and ideology, and the history of Africans in America, the slaves and their struggle, the Civil War and Abraham Lincoln, communism, and Vietnam; and she became more active by joining organizations and attending events specifically for black students.

When she joined the Republic of New Afrika, she was given the African name, Ybumi Oladele. It was at one of the organization's meetings that she met Mutulu Shakur (unrelated), who would later become one of the people involved in her escape from prison. At the

24

meetings they discussed the organization's three primary goals: 1) How to create an independent black-majority nation composed of Alabama, Georgia, Louisiana, Mississippi, and South Carolina, and the black-majority counties adjacent to these states in Arkansas, Texas, North Carolina, Tennessee and Florida; 2) Payment of several billion dollars in reparations to African-American descendants of slaves by the U.S. government; and 3) A referendum of all African Americans to determine their desires for citizenship since they were not offered a choice in this matter after emancipation in 1865 following the American Civil War.

In 1967, Assata was arrested for the first time with one hundred other Borough of Manhattan Community College students on charges of trespassing. The students had chained and locked the entrance to a college building to protest a curriculum deficient in black studies and a lack of black faculty.

A short time later, in April of that same year, she married Louis Chesimard who seemed to share her commitment to the Black Liberation struggle. However, the marriage only lasted until December 1970. She describes the brief relationship in her autobiography:

My husband was politically conscious, intelligent, and decent, and our affair was frantic, high-pitched, and charged with emotion. Somehow, I believed that our shared commitment to the Black Liberation struggle would result in a 'marriage made in heaven.' I spent most of my time at school, meetings, or demonstrations and whenever I was at home my head was usually stuck in some book. It was unthinkable to allow more than five minutes on mundane things like keeping house or washing dishes. To complicate matters, my husband's ideas about marriage stemmed mostly from his parents' life, where his mother was the homemaker and his father was the breadwinner. Spaghetti was about the only thing I could cook, and he was profoundly shocked to learn I had none of his mother's domestic skills. After a while, it became clear to me that I was about as ready to be married as I was to grow wings

and fly. So after a confused and unhappy year, we decided we made
much better friends than marriage partners and called it quits.

By now, Assata's aunt, Evelyn Williams, had given up private practice to set up a legal services program in Harlem under the auspices of African American Congressional Representative Adam Clayton Powell, Jr. In 1968 she became a supervising attorney for another pilot program, the New York University (NYU) Urban Affairs and Poverty Law Program. The next year she was appointed minority student adviser for NYU's Law School.

After Assata graduated from Manhattan Community College, she enrolled in City College of New York (CCNY), the oldest of City University's twenty-four institutions of higher learning and known for its political radicalism. Some claimed that CCNY made UCLA at Berkeley look conservative. Assata graduated at the age of 23 and then moved to California where she believed everything was happening, especially in the Bay area around Berkeley.

Once at Berkeley, she began reading about the theory of urban warfare as outlined by Argentine Marxist revolutionary and a major figure of the Cuban Revolution, Che Guevara, Brazilian Marxist revolutionary and writer, Carlos Mariguella, and the Tupamaros or MLN-T (*Movimiento de Liberación Nacional-Tupamaros*/Tupamaros National Liberation Movement), a left-wing urban guerrilla group in Uruguay. Revolution was no longer just for the blacks, Assata was discovering; it also involved white radicals, hippies, Latinos, Chicanos, and Asians.

As part of a first aid skills class, Assata worked as an assistant to a doctor who volunteered once a week at Alcatraz, and it was there that she learned about the Native Americans who were protesting against a long series of broken treaties, genocidal policies, and racist exploitation. She became involved with the Brown Berets, a pro-Chicano group that had been started in California and Texas that focused on returning all United States territory once held by Mexico to Mexico, and organized against police brutality as well as advocated for educational equality. She was also drawn to the Red Guard, a group of young men and women who were struggling in

Chinatown and San Francisco as part of the paramilitary social movement that had been mobilized by Mao Zedong during the Cultural Revolution. And, she began spending more and more of her time with a fledgling organization calling itself the Black Panther Party—she was learning from all of them.

Huey P. Newton and fellow activist Bobby Seals had established the Soul Students Advisory Council while students at Merritt Community College in Oakland, California. Its purpose was to help develop leadership; and then return to the black community and serve the black community in a revolutionary fashion. A short time later, in 1966 they organized the Black Panthers, heavily inspired by human rights leader and activist, Malcolm X, adopting from him the slain activist's slogan "freedom by any means necessary" as their own.

Founded and headquartered in Oakland, California, and renamed the Black Panther Party for Self Defense, the Party's goals, enumerated in its ten-point program and highlighted by a clenched fist, were to achieve equality and self-determination for black people. Among other things, the Party called for community control of institutions within the black community, such as schools and the police, an end to police brutality and murder, and an end to the military draft for black people.

In time, the BPP set up give-away programs whereby its members provided breakfasts to school age children, opened free health clinics, established legal aid offices and senior facilities, and demanded quality education for blacks. The Panthers also advocated the right to self-defense, including armed self-defense when under attack, even when that attack came from the police.

Within a year, there were approximately twenty-one chapters of the Black Panther Party with at least five hundred members nationwide. In New York City, Black Panther Party offices opened at 2026 Seventh Avenue and 108A Fulton Street, in Brooklyn. There were also chapters in the Bronx and Queens. After the assassination of Martin Luther King in 1968, Panther membership grew to 5000, with 49 chapters around the country.

Because of unresolved disagreements with Newton, Seals severed his relationship with the Panthers in 1974, thereby moving Eldridge Cleaver, who had been serving as Minister of Information and later head of the International Section of the Panthers, up in the chain of command. Cleaver had joined the Black Panther Party in 1967 while paroled on an assault charge, and soon became the voice of the activist group, coming up with attention-getting slogans and editing its newspaper. A serial rapist, he defended his violent actions against white women as being "insurrectionary" rapes, justified by what African Americans had suffered under a system dominated by whites. He writes in his book, *Soul on Ice:*

I became a rapist. To refine my technique and modus operandi, I started out by practicing on black girls in the ghetto — in the black ghetto where dark and vicious deeds appear not as aberrations or deviations from the norm, but as part of the sufficiency of the Evil of the day — and when I considered myself smooth enough, I crossed the tracks and sought out white prey. I did this consciously, deliberately, willfully, methodically — though looking back I see that I was in a frantic, wild and completely abandoned frame of mind.

Rape was an insurrectionary act. It delighted me that I was defying and trampling upon the white man's law, upon his system of values, and that I was defiling his women — and this point, I believe, was the most satisfying to me because I was very resentful over the historical fact of how the white man has used the black woman. I felt I was getting revenge.

In 1968, Cleaver ran for President of the United States of America on the Peace and Freedom Party ticket, nominated over Richard "Dick" Gregory by a margin of 161.5 to 54. Several different vice presidential nominees were considered as his running mate, including Chicago activist Peggy Terry, Chicano activist Rodolfo "Corky" Gonzales, radical economist Doug Dowd, and Judith Mage, president of the Social Service Employees Union who had been nominated at the national convention. Cleaver personally preferred Yippie leader Jerry Rubin. However, born in 1935, Cleaver didn't meet the requisite age requirement of thirty-five and was, therefore, disqualified. In spite of this, he received 36,571 votes.

A short while later, on April 6, following the assassination of Martin Luther King, Jr., Cleaver, along with thirteen other Panthers, led an ambush of Oakland police officers for the purpose of killing police officers. During the ambush at a house in West Oakland, two officers and Cleaver were wounded, and 17-year-old Black Panther member Bobby Hutton was killed. A year earlier, Hutton had become the first member and the first treasurer of the Black Panther Party. Charged with attempted murder, Cleaver jumped bail and fled to Cuba.

The BPP's militant advocacy for human rights and political empowerment alarmed the government, especially law enforcement. More often than not, the Panthers seemed to exist on a thin line between revolutionary and criminal activity. As a source of fund raising, some Panthers partnered with criminals to rob banks and deal drugs. They also killed one another. Particularly after the Newton-Cleaver split, criminality became more common.

In an effort to curtail the rapidly growing Black Panther Party, in 1967 then FBI Director J. Edgar Hoover initiated a plan—a counter intelligence program (COINTELPRO)—with a stated purpose to "expose, disrupt, and otherwise neutralize" the activities of black organizations, their members, and leaders. Within that context, the Black Panther Party was targeted as his primary scapegoat. Attorney General Robert F. Kennedy personally authorized some of these programs.

The most serious of the FBI disruption programs were those directed against "black nationalists." Agents were instructed to undertake actions to discredit these groups both within "the responsible Negro community" and the "Negro radicals," also "the white community, both the responsible community and to 'liberals' who have vestiges of sympathy for militant black nationalists simply because they are Negroes."

A March 4, 1968, memo from J. Edgar Hoover to FBI field offices laid out the goals of the COINTELPRO - Black Nationalist Hate Groups Program: "to prevent the coalition of militant black nationalist groups; to prevent the rise of a messiah who could unify and electrify the militant black nationalist movement; to prevent violence on the part of black nationalist groups; to prevent militant black nationalist groups and leaders from gaining respectability; and to prevent the long-range growth of militant black nationalist organizations, especially among youth." Among the targets of the program were a broad spectrum of civil rights and religious groups, such as the Ku Klux Klan, the Socialist Workers Party, and the Black Panther Party. Individuals targeted included Martin Luther King, Malcolm X, Stokely Carmichael, Elijah Muhammad, and Eldridge Cleaver.

The COINTELPRO operations were modeled on the successful programs of earlier years undertaken to disrupt the American Communist Party and were generally regarded as legitimate. The reasons behind the actions undertaken by the government to destroy the Black Panther Party are partially revealed in a June 1970 top secret Special Report for President Nixon. The report describes the Party as "the most active and dangerous black extremist group in the United States." Its "hard-core members" were estimated at about eight hundred, but "a recent poll indicates that approximately 25 percent of the black population has a great respect for the BPP, including 43 percent of blacks under 21 years of age." On the basis of such estimates, and taking into consideration the potential of the party, counterintelligence operations were carried out to ensure that it did not succeed in organizing as a substantial social or political force.

The same Special Report explains that "the movement of rebellious youth known as the 'New Left,' involving and influencing a substantial number of college students, is having a serious impact on contemporary society with a potential for serious domestic strife." It also states that "the major threat to the internal security of the United States is that directed against the civilian sector of our society."

The Black Panther Party, with its ten-point platform, had become the number one organization targeted by the FBI's COINTELPRO program. Because the Black Panther Party demanded the total liberation of black people, J. Edgar Hoover called it the "greatest threat to the internal security of the country" and vowed to destroy it along with its leaders and activists. It was at this time that Assata Shakur knew she wanted to be one of the people who stood up. She wanted to stand up for what she believed, for the black struggle. And she wanted to struggle on a full-time basis.

With the stated mission of COINTELPRO as her primary motivation, Assata Shakur went to New York and immediately joined the Black Panther Party located in Harlem on Seventh Avenue. That same evening, she was fully involved and on a bus to Philadelphia to attend the Party's plenary session for the constitutional convention that had been called for later in D.C. which would write a new antiracist and antifascist constitution guaranteeing the rights of the poor and oppressed.

Once back in New York she was assigned to the medical cadre responsible for the health care of the Panthers. Her immediate supervisor was Joan Victoria Bird, previously charged with the attempted murder of two policemen, and one of the defendants charged with conspiracy to blow up the New York Botanical Gardens, department stores, and police stations, among other things, in what became known as the New York Panther 21 case. Bird, along with the other Black Panther members awaiting trial in the New York Panther 21 case, who were the primary leadership of the eastern region of the Black Panther Party, would eventually be acquitted of all charges in what would become known as the longest political trial in New York's history.

After being a member for only a short while, Assata was expelled for breaking the rules when she left some Party papers at a meeting unattended, but was then reinstated and reassigned to help coordinate a school breakfast program in East Harlem. At this time, some of Assata's closest friends in the Party were Afeni Shakur (the mother of the late rapper Tupac Shakur), Dhoruba Bin-Wahad (co-founder of the Black Liberation Army), and Mumia Abu-Jamal (activist and journalist currently on death row at the State Correctional Institution – Mahanoy in Schuylkill County, Pennsylvania, for the 1981 murder of Philadelphia police officer Daniel Faulkner). All were out on bail from the Panther 21 case. And there was Zayd Malik Shakur, whom Assata considered her closest friend and comrade.

Assata continued to study Marx, Lenin, and Engels, Ho Chi Minh, Kim II Sung, Che, and Fidel, reading passages from Mao's *Red Book*, and articles published in the BPP paper, officially called the *Black Panther Party Intercommunal News Service*. But it was here that Assata began to separate from the Party. The Party members underestimated, in her opinion, the need to unite with other black organizations and to struggle around various community issues. It was her strong belief that it was the duty of black people to work in the black community—and that it was necessary for black, white, Hispanic, Native American, and Asian people to come together to fight. And although she was quick to give credit to the Black Panther Party for making it clear that the enemy was not the white people, but, rather, the capitalistic, imperialistic oppressors, her main two criticisms of the BPP were the macho behavior of males in the Party which caused constant internal bickering and unrest, and the Party's lack of focus on black history. She stated:

The basic problem stemmed from the fact that the BPP had no systematic approach to political education. They were reading the Red Book but didn't know who Harriet Tubman, Marcus Garvey, and Nat Turner were ... A whole lot of them barely understood any kind of history, Black, African or otherwise.

As Assata's aunt, Evelyn Williams, became more and more involved in working for change within the system to fight racism and institutionalized prejudice, Joey became increasingly involved in battling it from another angle. Assata soon left the Party, and, now divorced, that same year she joined the Black Liberation Army (BLA), an underground Black Panther Party splinter organization formed in response to COINTELPRO and often defined as "a radical and violent organization of black activists whose primary objective was to fight for the independence and self-determination of Afrikan people in the United States."

The *Philadelphia Inquirer* stated that the BLA wanted to instigate revolution by assassinating police. In an interview with the *Inquirer,* New York detective John Flynn said: "They figured that the police would overreact and attack the black community. When that happened, they assumed they would be able to enlist other blacks in their fight."

While worried about Joey's activities, Williams nevertheless trusted and supported her niece's decision. She writes in her autobiography, *Inadmissible Evidence: The Story of the African-American Trial Lawyer Who Defended the Black Liberation Army,* about her niece's political activism during this period: "I thought about the racism that had eroded the socialization process for African Americans, a process that is essential for all humans because it provides the structure within which all behavior is fashioned … I understood when a new generation of African Americans grew impatient with years of theoretical progress."

As a member of the Black Liberation Army, Assata began working with the "railroad" stations, a BLA underground support network that located the basic necessities for people and helped them get to where they wanted to go. Some of the members fled underground to avoid the COINTELPRO-inspired violence. Others chose to go underground to further revolutionary activity. It was Assata's belief that organizing small, armed, underground "strike teams" was the best way to continue resistance. Assata writes in her autobiography:

I wasn't one who believed that we should wait until our political struggle had reached a high point before we began to organize the underground. I felt it was important to start building underground structures as soon as possible. And although I felt that the major task of the underground should be organizing and building, I didn't feel that armed acts of resistance should be ruled out. As long as they didn't impede our long-range plans, guerrilla units should be

33

able to carry out a few well-planned, well-timed armed actions that were well coordinated with above-ground political objectives. Not any old kind of actions, but actions that black people would clearly understand and support and actions that were well publicized in the black community.

On May 19, 1971, NYPD officers Thomas Curry and Nicholas Binetti were seriously wounded by machine gun fire on Riverside Drive in Manhattan while guarding the home of Frank S. Hogan, the Manhattan district attorney. Two nights later, two other officers, Waverly Jones and Joseph Piagentini, were shot and killed outside a housing project in Harlem; and eight months following those murders, NYPD officers Gregory Foster and Rocco Laurie were killed on the Lower East Side as they walked their posts on Avenue B and East 11th Street. Other armed attacks occurred in California and elsewhere during this same period. In separate communiques delivered to the media, the Black Liberation Army claimed responsibility. In response, President Richard Nixon ordered a "full-out" law enforcement effort to capture former BPP members who might have been involved in the attacks.

Immediately after these shootings, the FBI made the investigation of these incidents part of their long-standing program against the BPP conducted by their "Racial Matters" squad, and set up a liaison with the NYPD. The initial joint FBI-NYPD investigation, an effort involving total cooperation and sharing of information, was called "Newkill" and later became a model for the Joint Terrorism Task Force and other agencies.

FBI agents involved in COINTELPRO now became part of Newkill. The FBI made all its facilities and resources, including its laboratory, available to the NYPD. Then NYPD Chief Inspector Michael Codd was assured of "complete" FBI cooperation. In turn, NYPD Chief of Detectives Albert Seedman, who coordinated the NYPD's investigation, ordered his subordinates to give the FBI "all available information developed to date, as well as in future investigations." The FBI and NYPD held regular conferences during which all parties were fully briefed. BPP members who were then underground as well as other extremist organizations, including the so-called Third World groups, were considered logical suspects and targeted for arrest.

Although the claimed purpose of the Bureau's COINTELPRO tactics was to prevent violence, some of the FBI's tactics against the BPP were clearly intended to foster violence, and many others could reasonably have been expected to cause violence. For example, the FBI's efforts to "intensify the degree of animosity" between the BPP and the Blackstone Rangers, a Chicago street gang, included sending an anonymous letter to the gang's leader falsely informing him that the Chicago Panthers had "a hit out" on him. The underlying intent of the letter was to induce the Ranger leader to "take reprisals against" the Panther leadership.

Similarly, in Southern California, the FBI launched a covert effort to "create further dissension in the ranks of the BPP." This effort included mailing anonymous letters and caricatures to BPP members ridiculing the local and national BPP leadership for the express purpose of exacerbating an existing gang war between the BPP and an organization called the United Slaves (US). This gang war resulted in the killing of four BPP members by members of US and in numerous beatings and shootings. Although individual incidents in this dispute cannot be directly traced to efforts by the Bureau, FBI officials were clearly aware of the violent nature of the dispute.

In 1971, in their ongoing efforts to cause dissention and increase tensions and factionalism within the BPP ranks, contradictions rising out of the acts of reform as opposed to revolution were perpetuated by COINTELPRO forces. This culminated in a split in the BPP leadership between Huey P. Newton and Eldridge Cleaver. Specifically, Cleaver advocated the escalation of armed resistance into urban guerilla warfare as a response to COINTELPRO and other actions by the government against the Black Panthers, while Newton suggested the best way to respond was to focus on more pragmatic reformist activity. It was his belief that the use of guns only served to alienate the Panthers from the rest of the black community.

While Cleaver went on to lead what came to be known as the Black Liberation Army, which had previously existed as the underground faction and fighting apparatus of the BPP, Newton, who was bipolar and had serious alcohol and drug addiction problems, continued leading the broken Black Panther Party in California. By the mid-1970s, Newton was accused of murdering a 17-year-old sex worker and assaulting a tailor. To avoid prosecution, he fled to Cuba in 1974, but returned to the U.S. three years later. The murder case was eventually dismissed after two trials ended with deadlocked juries, while the tailor refused to testify in court in relation to assault charges. Newton went on to earn a Ph.D. in social philosophy from the University of California, Santa Cruz, in 1980. In his final years, however, he faced legal prosecution and more prison time for weapons possession, financial misappropriations, and parole violations. Newton was shot and killed on a street in Oakland, California, in 1989 during a drug deal gone bad.

Prior to the split between Newton and Cleaver, the black underground was the official armed-wing of the aboveground political apparatus, and thereby had to maintain restraint in its military activity. As the Black Liberation Army under the leadership of Eldridge Cleaver, however, it became notorious for allegedly waging war against local police departments and using tactics of armed expropriations, sabotage, and ambush-assaults.

Assata aligned herself with the East Coast "Cleaver" (Eldridge Cleaver) faction, and though never formally a COINTELPRO target, she became a primary target of the FBIs anti-urban-terrorism investigations, collectively labeled under her name as "Chesrob," aimed at destroying BLA soldiers and their clandestine infrastructure. By mid-1971, many BPP members, particularly those from the East Coast, were "underground."

ɔʒ ꙮ

Chapter Three

HUNTING FOR JOANNE CHESIMARD

On April 6, 1971, Assata Shakur was shot in the stomach during a struggle with a guest at the Statler Hilton Hotel in Midtown Manhattan and taken to the hospital in fair condition. Once there, she was arrested and booked on charges of attempted robbery, felonious assault, reckless endangerment, and possession of a deadly weapon. Even though Assata refused to fully disclose the circumstances, a former Black Liberation Army member in New York said the incident stemmed from the BLA's attempts to intimidate and steal money from drug dealers. Assata confirmed that there was a drug connection, but would not elaborate. When she was released on bail, she is alleged to have said that she was glad she had been shot since now that she knew what that was like, she was no longer afraid to be shot again.

That summer, on August 23, 1971, Assata was sought for questioning in a bank robbery in Queens. A few months later, on December 21, 1971, she was identified along with Andrew Jackson, the man she was living with at the time in Atlanta, Georgia, from FBI photographs as a suspect in a hand grenade attack that destroyed a police car and slightly injured two patrolmen in Maspeth, Queens. Orders were issued to apprehend her. Assata describes what it was like to be under constant surveillance in her autobiography:

Everywhere I went it seemed like I would turn around to find two detectives following behind me. I would look out my window and there, in the middle of Harlem, in front of my house, would be two white men sitting and reading the newspaper. I was scared to death to talk in my own house.

In fear for her own life after seeing fellow activists killed by law enforcement and believing they had been framed, Bronx Black Panther JoAnne Chesimard followed her close friend Zayd Shakur underground. While in hiding, she changed her name; this time, to something meaningful to her. Even though JoAnne was the name her mother had given her, it no longer seemed to fit her African proclivity. And her married name, Chesimard, she believed had been the name of a slave master and adopted by her husband's ancestors. She considered keeping Ybumi Oladele, the name she was given when she joined the Republic of New Afrika as a student at Manhattan Community College, but she didn't know what it meant. She wanted a name that didn't sound white, yet had something to do with struggle and the liberation of her people. She decided on Assata (she who struggles), Olugbala (love for the people), Shakur (the thankful—out of respect for her friend, Zayd, and Zayd's family).

In 1972 Assata was wanted for questioning regarding a police officer being wounded while attempting to serve a traffic summons in Brooklyn, and again later when Msgr. John Powis alleged that she was involved in an armed robbery at his Our Lady of the Presentation Church in Brownsville, Brooklyn, based on FBI photographs. He later would recount the events to reporter Ron Robbins in an interview for VillageVoice.com:

Among the radicals was a trio who arrived at Presentation one evening asking Powis to write a letter for a job-seeking relative just out of jail. "I look up and they have three .45 automatics pointed at me." He was ordered to open the church safe with its $1,800 in bingo money. "Twice I couldn't open it. One of them says, 'We usually just blow the heads off white men.'" The safe finally complied. Powis was gagged, hooded, and locked in a bathroom. When the police arrived, they showed him pictures of likely suspects. He recognized one of the robbers. It was Black Liberation Army leader JoAnne Chesimard, a/k/a Assata Shakur. "I didn't know her, but I had heard that a few weeks before she and others had robbed and killed a white real estate broker on Howard Avenue. I guess I was lucky."

By now, the media had labeled Assata Shakur the "soul" of the Black Liberation Army, even claiming she was the *de facto* leader of the BLA following the arrest of co-founder Dhoruba al-Mujahid bin Wahad (born Richard Earl Moore).

Wahad had initially been arrested and charged with robbing a South Bronx social club, but was later charged with the attempted murders of NYPD officers Curry and Binetti. Two years and three trials later, he received a guilty verdict and was sentenced to twenty-five years to life.

Dhoruba Wahad would spend a total of nineteen years in prison. The one hour "Passin' It On" documentary by Jon Valadez on Dhoruba Wahad's case revealed, through FBI documents and eye witness accounts, that the South Bronx social club was running an illegal drug ring and was a known place where police took bribes. Before his arrest, Wahad and other BLA members attempted to stop the drugs being pushed into their neighborhood, but this information wouldn't come out until later.

While incarcerated, Wahad filed a lawsuit against the FBI and the police department of the City of New York. As a direct result of his lawsuit, over the next fifteen years the FBI released more than 300,000 pages of documents regarding COINTELPRO, the basis on which Wahad appealed his conviction. On March 15, 1990, Judge Peter J. McQuillan of the New York Supreme Court in Manhattan reversed the conviction, ruling that the prosecution had "failed to disclose evidence that could have helped Mr. Wahad's defense."

Meanwhile, the FBI was calling Assata Shakur the "revolutionary mother hen" of a Black Liberation Army cell that had conducted a "series of cold-blooded murders of New York City police officers." In June 1973, the FBI's Joint Terrorism Task Force began issuing daily briefings on Assata's status and the allegations against her, and collaborating in stakeouts that were the result of intensive political repression and counterintelligence campaigns like Newkill and Chesrob. (This same Joint Terrorism Task Force would later serve as the "coordinating body in the search for Assata and the renewed campaign to smash the BLA" after her escape from prison.)

Then, on May 2, 1973, around 12:45 a.m., Assata Shakur was riding in the front passenger's seat of a white Pontiac LeMans with Vermont license plates on the New Jersey Turnpike. Sundiata Acoli was driving, and Zayd Malik Shakur, former information minister for a New York faction of the Black Panthers, was a passenger in the backseat behind Assata.

In East Brunswick, State Trooper James Harper #2108 called in a motor vehicle stop— "an early 1960 (white) Pontiac, 2-door; occupied by two black males and one black female." He pulled the car over at milepost 83 for a broken tail light. According to the testimony of New Jersey State Police Col. David B. Kelly presented during the trial, the vehicle was also slightly exceeding the speed limit.

State Trooper Harper then radioed for backup. Trooper Ronald Foster #2240 was working the station record and serving as dispatcher. "I radioed to Bob Palentchar to back up Harper," recalled Foster in an interview with author John O'Rourke for his book *Jersey Troopers*, "but he did not answer and Werner picked up the call."

Meanwhile, in questioning the driver, Trooper Harper noted a discrepancy in the registration and asked Acoli to get out of the car and stand behind it. When Trooper Harper asked for Assata Shakur's identification, she said her name was Maurine Jones.

Trooper Werner Foerster #2608 in a second patrol vehicle (Car 820) arrived on the scene within minutes, followed a short time later by Trooper Robert Palentchar #1946 (Car 817).

David Krajicek, writer for the *New York Daily News,* describes what followed:

When Trooper Werner Foerster arrived, Harper left Squire (Sundiata Acoli) with him and went to the Pontiac to seek identification from Chesimard (Assata Shakur), who was riding in the front seat on the passenger side, and Costan (Zayd Shakur) in the backseat. Foerster found a gun clip while frisking Squire. As the trooper shouted a warning to his colleague, Chesimard pulled a gun and began shooting, hitting Harper in the left shoulder.

Harper ran for cover behind his radio car. He said he saw Squire and Trooper Foerster wrestling on the ground as both Chesimard and Costan fired handguns. Harper shot both passengers, then ran to the police office in the Turnpike Building for help, one-tenth of a mile away. (Testimony during the trial would reveal that Trooper Harper reported the shoot-out to Sergeant Chester Baginski who was in charge of maintaining the official record of turnpike occurrences in what was referred to as the "Station Bible.")

Squire then drove the Pontiac—which contained Assata Shakur, who was wounded, and Zayd Shakur, who was dead or dying—5 miles down the road at milepost 78 across from Service Area 8-N (the Joyce Kilmer Service Area). The vehicle was chased by three patrol cars and the booths down the turnpike were alerted. Squire then exited the car and—after being ordered to halt by Trooper Robert Palentchar (Car 817), the first on the scene—fled into the woods as Palentchar emptied his gun.

According to Palentchar, Assata Shakur, who apparently had been hiding in the grass, stood up, then walked towards him from 50 feet away with her bloody arms raised in surrender. Assata would claim that Acoli had carried her to the grass, afraid that the troopers would simply open fire on the get-away car if she were in it. Later, however, she changed her story, claiming that she was dragged from the car and thrown to the ground and stomped on. A short distance away, the trooper found Zayd Shakur's body in a ditch. The pistol belonging to Trooper Foerster was found in the escape vehicle.

Back at the shooting scene, Trooper O'Rourke, who had left the Administration building to investigate the scene of the shoot-out less than 200 yards away, found the body of Trooper Foerster, 34, a husband, father of a three-year-old son, and a Vietnam veteran, from Old Bridge, New Jersey, shot dead. Nearly an hour had passed from the time of the shooting since neither Harper nor Palentchar reported that Foerster had been on the scene and involved in the shootout. Evidence would reveal he took four bullets, including two in the head, shot execution style from his own gun. Two jammed handguns were recovered at the original shooting scene, authorities said, and two more were found near the abandoned car. Next to Foerster's body, authorities also found a wallet containing the identification papers of Archie Gibson, from Brooklyn.

In his testimony, Kelly explained that the car had been coming from New York and was filled with false identification papers, including passports, birth certificates and Social Security cards. There also were three books on black liberation, including one entitled *Beat the Heat—A Radical Survival Handbook.* Another contained a list of potential BLA targets.

Less than a half hour before the shooting, the three had stopped for snacks at Howard Johnson's restaurant, Alexander Hamilton rest area, near Newark on the Turnpike, police learned from witnesses. Two nearly-empty bags of Howard Johnson-brand popcorn and potato chips were among the items taken from the car and "dusted" by New York City fingerprint expert Michael Kean.

The fugitive driver of the car was described as a six-foot, 180-pound black man wearing a white or tan safari jacket and a brown fedora with a gold chain in it. At 5:15 a.m., he was believed to have been sighted in nearby Milltown, and fearing that he might have hidden in one of the houses, state and local police ordered a house-to-house search of the community of 6,800 residents.

The car, described as white but with one dark maroon door, was registered to Isabelle Johnson, of Pine St., Bennington, Vt., but Motor Vehicles authorities in that state said there was no such address. They also reported that on Monday someone had paid cash for a duplicate copy of the registration. Their records indicated that the car had first been licensed in Vermont on Dec. 29, 1972, and was acquired in New Jersey from someone named "Hollinger" on Oct. 27, 1972. The registration number, as listed there, was 1166A, Vermont.

After a thirty-six-hour manhunt the next day involving four hundred people, state police helicopters, and bloodhounds from the Ocean County Sheriff's Department, Sundiata Acoli was captured within a mile of their car at milepost 78 south. Acoli describes his capture:

When i was arrested, police immediately cut my pants off me so that i only wore shorts. Whooping and hollering, a gang of New Jersey state troopers dragged me through the woods, through water puddles, and hit me over the head with the barrel of their shot gun. They only cooled out somewhat when they noticed that all the commotion had caused a crowd to gather at the edge of the road, observing their actions.

Zayd Shakur's body, found in a nearby gully along the road a few feet from where Assata Shakur surrendered, was later identified through his fingerprints from two previous arrests in 1961 and 1970; one for grand larceny and another for weapons' violations, for which actress Jane Fonda arranged bail, claiming that she knew him.

Fonda was one of several Hollywood entertainers and other celebrities, including Marlon Brando and Leonard Bernstein, who were sympathetic of the Black Liberation Army's cause and supported its goals. In retaliation, in June 1970, FBI headquarters had approved an anonymous letter informing Hollywood gossip columnist, Army Archerd, that actress Jane Fonda had appeared at a BPP fund-raising function, noting: "It can be expected that Fonda's involvement with the BPP cause could detract from her status with the general public if reported in a Hollywood 'gossip column.'" The letter was never printed.

In 1975, the FBI once again attempted to use the *Daily Variety* gossip column by funneling false information to Archerd, suggesting that left-leaning actress Jane Fonda had threatened President Nixon's life at the Embassy Auditorium where she was speaking on behalf of the Black Panther Defense Fund. Fonda had been pursuing a $2.8 million civil rights suit against the government since 1973 involving wire taps, tax audits, mail covers, and, on an even more personal level, determining when Fonda would give birth to her unborn child.

Archerd, though, wasn't fooled, and the next issue of *Variety* carried the shocking banner headline, "FBI Jane Fonda lie fizzles." In an interview with *Daily Variety*, Fonda said that the FBI memos supported her charges that the Nixon administration organized a campaign to discredit her political activities. Further, she added, "Those of us who opposed the Nixon administration were being made to appear irresponsible, dangerous and foul-mouthed," denying making any threats against Nixon's life.

Following the turnpike shootout, according to a New Jersey Police spokesperson, Assata Shakur was on her way to a "new hideout in Philadelphia," and "heading ultimately for Washington." Shakur, however, testified that she was on her way to Baltimore for a job as a bar waitress.

Trooper Harper, wounded in the left shoulder, was taken to Middlesex General Hospital in good condition and given a protective guard at the hospital. With gunshot wounds in both arms and a shoulder, Assata Shakur was also taken to Middlesex General Hospital under heavy guard and was reported to be in serious condition. Assata refused to identify herself, but her fingerprints matched those on an FBI flyer listing her, Joanne Deborah Chesimard, as wanted for a bank robbery.

As a team of ten troopers, each armed with shotguns, stood on guard outside of her room, Assata chanted repeatedly, "If I had some poison gas, I'd throw it on your white ass." She was interrogated and arraigned from her hospital bed, then transferred from Middlesex General Hospital in New Brunswick to Roosevelt

Hospital in Edison after her lawyers obtained a court order from Judge John Bachman. A few weeks later, she was transferred to Middlesex County Workhouse and eventually taken to Rikers Island Correctional Institution for Women in New York City.

Both Acoli and Shakur claimed to have been set up in the traffic stop. Both denied shooting Trooper Foerster.

The Pontiac LeMans and Trooper Harper's patrol car were taken to a state police garage in East Brunswick. Following the incident, on May 11, the State Police instituted two-man night patrols on the turnpike and Garden State Parkway, although the change was not made public until June.

More than 3,000 policemen from law enforcement agencies around the country attended the funeral of Werner Foerster in East Brunswick, New Jersey. In November 2014, forty-two years later, New Jersey State officials dedicated a monument in remembrance of State Trooper Foerster. "We honor him, we honor his family," Colonel Rick Fuentes said at the dedication held at the old New Jersey Turnpike Authority building off Route 18, near the site where Foerster was killed in the line of duty. In addition to Col. Rick Fuentes, Lt. Col. Patrick Callahan, Troop "D" Commander Eric Heitmann, Acting Attorney General John J. Hoffman and others participated in the dedication ceremony.

This was the second memorial honoring Trooper Foerster. In 2005, a sign was unveiled marking the Turnpike overpass on Route 18 in East Brunswick as a memorial to Foerster. His name is also included in a "Remembering the Fallen" memorial honoring 27 police officers who have died in the line of duty in Middlesex County since 1856. The memorial, displayed at the Middlesex County Police Training Center in Edison, has a mural listing the name and agency of each officer. A booklet next to the mural contains the biographical information and circumstance of each officer's death.

 os so

Barbara Casey

Chapter Four

THE TRIALS

Assata Shakur was indicted ten times between 1973 and 1977, in New York and New Jersey, resulting in seven different criminal trials. She was charged with two bank robberies, the kidnapping of a Brooklyn heroin dealer, attempted murder of two Queens' police officers stemming from a January 23, 1973, failed ambush, and eight other felonies related to the turnpike shootout. Of these trials, three indictments were dismissed without trial; three resulted in acquittals, one in a hung jury, one in a change of venue, and one in a mistrial due to pregnancy. Only one, the New Jersey Turnpike shootout, resulted in a conviction.

For two years leading up to the capture of her niece, Evelyn Williams and her family had been surveilled by the FBI and lived in fear that Assata would be killed in a shootout with police, as some other members of the BLA had been. Williams describes what it was like during that time:

It was the spring of 1973 and for the last two years the nationwide dragnet for her capture had intensified each time a young

African American identified as a member of the BLA was arrested or wounded or killed. The Joint Terrorist Task Force, made up of the FBI and local police agencies across the country, issued daily bulletins predicting her imminent apprehension each time another bank had been robbed or another cop had been killed. Whenever there was a lull in such occurrences, they leaked information, allegedly classified as 'confidential,' to the media, repeating past accusations and flashing her face across television screens and newspapers with heartbeat regularity, lest the public forget.

When Assata was captured and taken into custody in early May of 1973, and authorities began issuing criminal charges against her and other BLA members, Williams quit her job as a minority student advisor and law instructor to become Shakur's defense attorney.

The first order of business was to attend to Assata's legal and medical rights. Regarding Assata's medical needs, Williams' family feared that Assata was not receiving proper medical treatment for the gunshot wounds she sustained during the turnpike shootout. As far as Williams' legal concerns, at first Williams was not permitted private conferences with her client in order to plan a defense strategy. This was one of several fundamental constitutional rights that Assata Shakur was denied, according to Williams, which she fought to achieve over the next few years in a legal quagmire involving the prosecutorial arms of the States of New York and New Jersey, as well as the Federal Bureau of Investigation. In her book, *Inadmissible Evidence: The Story of the African-American Trial Lawyer Who Defended the Black Liberation Army*, Williams writes of the injustice faced by Shakur and the other members of the BLA, "and the difficult years for all participants as the cases dragged on; Shakur was incarcerated in often inhumane conditions," while Williams "faced a wall of institutionalized racism that seemed bent on locking up my niece for good if it could not eliminate her permanently."

In the series of New York and New Jersey trials that began in 1973, Williams defended Assata successfully on a number of charges, claiming the charges were trumped up for the intention of defusing the political threat posed by the BLA. However, Assata didn't make it easy for her aunt/attorney. Outside of court, she complained that Williams wasn't doing enough or wasn't doing it quickly enough, and ignoring Assata's wishes and demands. Her complaints continued during the trials as well as Assata repeatedly disrupted court proceedings, yelling profanities and threats, spitting, refusing to stand when the judge entered the courtroom, and performing other acts of disrespect toward the court.

One judge threatened to have her bound and gagged, and ordered the case to proceed without her being present. Williams, however, refused to continue with the trial unless her client was in court. This resulted in Williams being charged with contempt of court and ordered to serve ten days in jail. Williams was taken in handcuffs to the jail where she imposed a hunger strike on herself for the duration of the ten-day prison stay. "Being a lawyer for a political prisoner is in no way comparable to representing the usual criminal defendant," writes Williams in her book. "While occasionally they are forced to do so, they usually will not conform to the rules of the court, to the rules of criminal or civil procedure, or to the rules of evidence, not to mention the rules of prescribed courtroom decorum .... And they refuse to be deterred by fear of the systems' retaliatory might or by the hope that submission to its rules would benefit them."

In December 1973, Assata Shakur, along with co-defendant Kamau Sadiki (born Fred Hilton), was tried for a September 29, 1972, $3,700 robbery of the Manufacturers Hanover Trust Company in the Bronx. Prior to this, on November 3, 1971, Sadiki was suspected of killing Atlanta Police Officer James Green while on patrol in his police van at a closed gas station. However, with no physical evidence implicating Sadiki, the Atlanta Police Department closed the Atlanta case as unsolved.

In light of the pending murder prosecution against Assata Shakur in New Jersey State Court, her lawyer, Evelyn Williams, requested that the Bronx trial be postponed for six months to permit further preparation. Sadiki's lawyer, Robert Bloom, at first requesting to have the trial dismissed, then asked for a postponement due to new "revelations" regarding the credibility of one of the witnesses, Avon White, a former co-defendant working for the prosecution. Bloom had been assigned to defend Hilton over the summer, but White was not disclosed as a government witness until right before the trial. Judge Lee Gagliardi denied both the dismissal and the postponement, and the Second Circuit denied Assata Shakur's petition for a writ of mandamus. In protest, the lawyers Williams and Bloom stayed mute, and Shakur and Sadiki conducted their own defense.

The prosecution's case rested largely on the testimony of two men who had pleaded guilty to participating in the holdup. The four witnesses called were Avon White and John Rivers, both of whom had already been convicted of the robbery, and the manager and teller of the bank. Even though White and Rivers had already been convicted, they had been told the charges would be dropped if they testified that Shakur had guarded one of the doors with a .357 magnum pistol and Sadiki had served as a lookout and drove the getaway truck.

Since the defense was protesting and, therefore, not participating in the trial, neither White nor Rivers were cross-examined. Both defendants, Assata Shakur and Kamau Sadiki, were cited repeatedly for contempt of court and eventually barred from the courtroom and placed in a holding room. Evelyn Williams was also cited for contempt, and the trial was delayed for a few days after Assata was diagnosed with pleurisy, an inflammation of the lining surrounding the lungs.

Both the defense and the prosecution were instructed by Judge Gagliardi not to bring up Shakur's or Sadiki's connections to the BLA, stating that the information was "not relevant." Gagliardi also denied the jurors' requests to ask questions either directly of the witnesses or through him, and declined to provide the jury with information about how long the defense had been given to prepare, telling them it was "none of their concern." The trial resulted in a hung jury and then a mistrial when the jury reported to Gagliardi that they were deadlocked for the fourth time.

At one point, Evelyn Williams asked to be relieved of her duties due to disagreements with Hilton's attorney and her niece, Assata vocally unhappy with Williams' efforts on her behalf and not doing things the way she, the defendant, wanted them done. Williams' request was denied, but Judge Arnold Bauman directed another lawyer, Howard Jacobs, to defend Assata while Williams remained the attorney of record. The retrial, under Judge Bauman, was delayed for one day in order to give the defendants more time to prepare.

During jury selection, Assata Shakur's loud, disruptive behavior escalated, and she was ejected from the court room following another argument with Williams. Hilton was also removed from the court room, and the two defendants were confined to a padded, sound-proof holding room where they listened to the court proceedings through loud speakers. After the selection of twelve jurors (sixty were excused), Williams was allowed to retire from the case, with Shakur officially representing herself, assisted by lawyer, activist, and civil rights advocate Florynce Kennedy, whose intersectionality protest strategy was "mak(ing) white people nervous."

As in the previous trial, both defendants were thrown out of the court room for various periods of time because of their disruptions. The defense attempted to discredit White on the grounds he had spent eight months in New York's Matteawan Hospital for the Criminally Insane in 1968, to which he said he had faked insanity by claiming to be Allah in order to get transferred out of prison. He also admitted, under examination by Assata, that he had once been in love with her. To add to the confusion, one of the jurors who had been frequently napping during the trial was replaced with an alternate.

Both defendants were acquitted in the retrial; six of the jurors interviewed after the trial stated they did not believe the two key prosecution witnesses. Assata Shakur was immediately returned to Morristown, New Jersey, under heavy guard. Louis Chesimard, Assata's ex-husband, and Paul Stewart, the other two alleged robbers, already had been acquitted in June.

On the charges related to the New Jersey Turnpike shootout, New Jersey Superior Court Judge Leon Gerofsky had ordered a change of venue several months earlier from Middlesex to Morris County, New Jersey, saying "it was almost impossible to obtain a jury here comprised of people willing to accept the responsibility of impartiality so that defendants will be protected from transitory passion and prejudice." Polls of residents in Middlesex County, where Acoli had been convicted less than three years prior, showed that 83 percent knew Assata Shakur's identity and 70 percent said she was guilty.

Now, with the acquittal in the Bronx bank robbery trial, the New Jersey Turnpike shootout proceedings continued with Judge John E. Bachman in Middlesex County. The jury was chosen from Morris County, which had a far smaller black population than Middlesex County, the basis on which Assata attempted unsuccessfully to remove the trial to Federal Court.

Originally, Shakur was slated to be tried with Acoli, but before jury selection was complete, the trials were separated when it was learned that Assata was pregnant, having conceived in a holding room of the Bronx jail. The father was Fred Hilton, her co-defendant in the bank robbery trial. When describing her thoughts leading up to her pregnancy, Assata writes:

I am about life ... I'm gonna live as hard as i can and as full as i can until i die. And i'm not letting these parasites, these oppressors, these greedy racist swine make me kill my children in my mind, before they are even born. I'm going to live and i'm going to love Kamau, and, if a child comes from that union, i'm going to rejoice.

The pregnancy resulted in a mistrial in 1974 for Assata because of the possibility of miscarriage. She wouldn't be retried until three years later.

During this time, Assata Shakur had been receiving mail from all over the country, most of it from supporters. In response, she made a tape called "To My People," which was broadcast via radio on July

4, 1973. In her speech she called herself a black revolutionary and denounced what she believed was hypocrisy in the U.S. legal system:

My name is Assata Shakur (slave name joanne chesimard), and i am a revolutionary. A black revolutionary. By that i mean that i have declared war on all forces that have raped our women, castrated our men, and kept our babies empty-bellied.

Every revolution in history has been accomplished by actions, although words are necessary. We must create shields that protect us and spears that penetrate our enemies. Black people must learn how to struggle by struggling. We must learn by our mistakes.

In her view, the police and the courts had established double standards based on race and were treating black Americans unjustly, purely because of their color. She concludes her statement as follows:

There is, and always will be, until every black man, woman, and child is free, a Black Liberation Army. The main function of the Black Liberation Army at this time is to create good examples, to struggle for black freedom, and to prepare for the future. We must defend ourselves and let no one disrespect us. We must gain our liberation by any means necessary.

On December 31, 1973, Assata Shakur and four others, including Fred Hilton, Avon White, and Andrew Jackson, were indicted in the State Supreme Court in the Bronx on charges of attempting to shoot and kill two policemen—Michael O'Reilly and Roy Polliana—in a January 28, 1973, ambush in St. Albans, Queens. O'Reilly and Polliana were both wounded, but had since returned to duty. On April 26, 1974, while Assata Shakur was pregnant, and even though on March 5, 1974, two new defendants (Jeannette Jefferson and Robert Hayes) were named in an indictment involving the same charges, New Jersey Governor Brendan Byrne signed an extradition order to move Assata to New York to face two counts of attempted murder, attempted assault, and possession of dangerous weapons related to the alleged ambush. However, Assata declined to waive her right to an extradition hearing and asked for a full hearing before Middlesex County Court Judge John E. Backman.

Assata Shakur was extradited to New York City on May 6, arraigned on May 11 after pleading innocent, and remanded to jail by Justice Albert S. McGrover of the State Supreme Court pending a pretrial hearing on July 2. In November 1974, New York State Supreme Court Justice Peter Farrell dismissed the attempted murder indictment because of insufficient evidence, declaring, "The court can only note with disapproval that virtually a year has passed before counsel made an application for the most basic relief permitted by law, namely an attack on the sufficiency of the evidence submitted by the grand jury."

On May 30, 1974, Assata was indicted on the charge of having robbed a Brooklyn bar and kidnapping bartender James E. Freeman for ransom. Assata and co-defendant Ronald Myers were accused of entering the bar with pistols and shotguns, taking $50 from the register, kidnapping the bartender, leaving a note demanding a $20,000 ransom from the bar owner, and fleeing in a rented truck. Acting as her own co-counsel, Assata stated in her opening remarks to Judge William Thompson and the jurors:

I have decided to act as co-counsel, and to make this opening statement, not because I have any illusions about my legal abilities, but, rather, because there are things that I must say to you .... I do not think that it's an accident we are on trial here. This case is just another example of what has been going on in this country. Throughout amerika's history, people have been imprisoned because of their political beliefs and charged with criminal acts in order to justify the imprisonment.

Assata Shakur and co-defendant Ronald Myers were acquitted on December 19, 1975, after seven hours of jury deliberation, ending a three-month trial in front of Judge William Thompson.

In July 1973, Assata Shakur had pleaded not guilty in Federal Court in Brooklyn to an indictment related to an August 31, 1971, $7,700 robbery of the Bankers Trust Company in Queens. After being indicted by a grand jury, Judge Jacob Mishlerset set a tentative trial date of November 5 of that year. The trial was delayed until 1976, and

Assata was to be represented by Evelyn Williams. However, another case Williams had taken in order to earn some money was ready for trial and couldn't be delayed any longer. Therefore, Assata hired Stanley Cohen, and she once again acted as her own co-counsel, just as she had in the Manufacturers Hanover Trust Company case and the Brooklyn bar robbery and kidnapping case.

Unlike the previous trials, this one had a carnival atmosphere about it, and the courtroom was packed with blacks supporting Shakur. The prosecution showed surveillance photos of four of the six alleged robbers, contending one of them was Shakur wearing a wig. When the judge ordered that Assata be photographed by the FBI, she refused to cooperate, believing that the FBI would use photo manipulation to prove her guilt. She was then forcibly subdued by law officials and photographed with her hair held back. In her autobiography, Assata recounts being beaten, choked, and kicked on the courtroom floor by five marshals, while Williams narrated the events to ensure they would appear in the court record.

A subsequent judge determined that the manner in which the photos were taken violated Assata's rights and ruled the new photos inadmissible. Shortly after deliberation began, the jury asked to see all the photographic exhibits taken from the surveillance footage, and determined that the FBI photo allegedly showing Assata Shakur participating in the robbery was not her. In addition, even though one bank employee testified that Assata was one of the bank robbers, two other employees, both bank tellers, testified they were uncertain, while the bank manager stated Assata Shakur was not the woman who robbed the bank.

Assata Shakur was acquitted after seven hours of jury deliberation on January 16, 1976. She was the only one of the six suspects in the robbery to be brought to trial. Andrew Jackson and two others indicted for the same robbery pleaded guilty: Jackson was sentenced to five years in prison and five years of probation; another was shot and killed in a gun fight in Florida on December 31, 1971; and the last remained at large at the time of Assata Shakur's acquittal.

Assata writes in her autobiography of that moment when the verdict was read:

A verdict had been reached. I could tell what it was before we even entered the courtroom. The pigs were upset, to put it mildly. The female guard who escorted me to kourt every day seemed glad. The jury read the verdict. Acquittal. The courtroom broke into a loud cheer. The judge just gave up calling for order. He had to wait for the shouting to die down. It was a long time coming. All the spectators were jumping around hugging each other.

In spite of her pregnancy, and the efforts of her attorneys filing "one civil rights lawsuit after another complaining of the barbarous treatment selectively meted out to her," Assata Shakur's living conditions in prison did not improve. In her autobiography, Assata denies that she shot at anyone and claims that the militant and cop-killer labels put on her that day of the New Jersey Turnpike shootout started a pattern of mistreatment and neglect by authorities that would continue throughout her incarceration. Months in solitary confinement, bright, blinding lights kept on 24 hours a day, freezing temperatures in her cell, and given food that was inedible, as well as the physical and verbal abuse, were some of the complaints Assata's lawyers were trying to remedy.

Even though she had her own doctor—Dr. Garrett, the courts insisted that a doctor they had appointed be present for all visits. When she went into labor, there was the problem that Dr. Garrett wasn't the court-appointed doctor and Assata was a prisoner. An impromptu demonstration was held outside the hospital in support of Assata being able to choose her own doctor, and Assata's lawyer, Evelyn Williams, and Dr. Garrett held a hastily-called news conference. After Assata signed a waiver relieving the hospital of any responsibility, Dr. Garrett was allowed to deliver the baby, and on September 11, 1974, she gave birth to her daughter, Kakuya Amala Olugbala Shakur, at the fortified psychiatric ward at Elmhurst General Hospital in Queens. A few days later, Assata Shakur was returned under heavy guard to Rikers Island; and custody of the baby was given to Shakur's mother, Evelyn Williams' sister, in New York.

On January 29 Assata Shakur was remanded back to New Jersey for the turnpike shootout trial. While awaiting trial, which wouldn't take place for more than a year, she was held in solitary confinement at the Middlesex County Jail for men.

While Assata awaited trial in the basement of the Middlesex County Jail, Lennox Hinds, then the head of the National Conference of Black Lawyers, together with the other members of her defense team, filed another civil suit against the State, once again charging that the conditions in which Assata Shakur was kept were inhumane and cruel.

Eventually a hearing officer named Ploshnik was appointed by the State and assigned to review Assata's jail conditions. He ruled that her imprisonment was indeed inhumane and recommended that they be changed immediately. Through a series of appeals and legal maneuvers, however, the State succeeded in keeping Assata in solitary confinement.

CB EO

Chapter Five

THE TURNPIKE SHOOTOUT TRIAL

Assata Shakur's murder trial for the turnpike shootout took place in New Brunswick, Middlesex County, New Jersey, not far from the site of the gunfight in East Brunswick. By the time Assata was again tried in 1977, Acoli had already been convicted of firing the bullets that killed Foerster and transferred to Trenton State Prison (TSP) for life plus thirty years consecutive in 1974. He was subsequently confined to a new and specially created Management Control Unit (MCU) created for him and other politically associated prisoners. Even with the conviction of Acoli, Assata Shakur would claim in a 2000 interview with *EMERGE* that "the gun that shot Werner Foerster was found under the body of Zayd Malik Shakur, in his hand. Blood was on the trigger." Other reports would have the gun found under Zayd Malik Shakur's leg.

At the time of Assata Shakur's trial, she was accused of being an accomplice in the murders of New Jersey State Trooper Werner Foerster and Zayd Shakur, the possession of weapons, and the assault and attempted murder of Harper. During the trial, hundreds of civil rights campaigners and Shakur supporters demonstrated outside of the

Middlesex County courthouse each day. The United States District Court for the State of New Jersey denied Assata's request to remove the trial to Federal Court. This was affirmed by an *en banc* panel of the United States Court of Appeals for the Third Circuit. Assata's attorneys did, however, successfully ask a ten-judge panel of the United States Court of Appeals for the Third Circuit to order that sessions for her murder trial not be held on Fridays because of Black Muslim Sabbath, Assata's religion of choice through the encouragement of Kamau Sadiki.

The nine-week trial was widely publicized throughout the United States, and was even reported on by the Telegraph Agency of the Soviet Union (TASS). By now, Assata had amassed a defense team that included Stanley Cohen, Lennox Hinds, Florynce Kennedy, Louis Myers, Laurence Stern, and Evelyn Williams. William Kunstler became involved in Assata's trials in 1975, when contacted by Williams, and commuted from New York City to New Brunswick every day with Stern. He was almost dismissed after telling a reporter that Shakur's jail conditions were "adequate," but then became the lead attorney for the defense team. Of these attorneys, Kunstler, Ball, Cohen, Myers, Stern and Williams appeared in court for the turnpike trial.

A total of 408 jurors were questioned during the *voir dire*, which concluded on February 14. All of the fifteen jurors—ten women and five men—were white, and most were under thirty years old. Five jurors had personal ties to State Troopers (one girlfriend, two nephews, and two friends). A sixteenth female juror was removed before the trial formally opened when it was determined that Sheriff Joseph DeMarino of Middlesex County, while a private detective several years earlier, had worked for a lawyer who represented the juror's husband. Judge Theodore Appleby repeatedly denied Kunstler's requests for DeMarino to be removed from his responsibilities for the duration of the trial "because he did not divulge his association with the juror."

One prospective juror was dismissed for reading *Target Blue,* a book by Robert Daley, a former New York City Deputy Police

Commander, which dealt in part with Shakur and had been left in the jury assembly room. Before the jury entered the courtroom, Judge Appleby ordered Shakur's lawyers to remove a copy of *Roots: The Saga of an American Family* by Alex Haley from the defense counsel table where it was easily visible to jurors. The *Roots* TV miniseries adopted from the book and shown shortly before the trial was believed to have evoked feelings of "guilt and sympathy" with many white viewers.

In the thirteen-minute opening statement by Edward J. Barone, the first assistant Middlesex County prosecutor directing the case for the State, he contended that Assata Shakur shot and killed her companion, Zayd Shakur, and "executed" Trooper Foerster with his own weapon. William Kunstler, the head of Assata's defense staff, moved immediately for a mistrial, calling the eight-count grand jury indictment an "adversary proceeding solely and exclusively under the control of the prosecutor," whom Kunstler accused of "improper prejudicial remarks." Judge Theodore Appleby, noting with irritation the frequent defense interruptions that had characterized the previous days' jury selection, denied the motion.

The next day, the jury listened to New Jersey State Police radio tapes while being provided with a printed transcript. Part of the tape, made after the wounded Harper entered the administration building near the site of the shootout, revealed the State Police radio operator, Trooper Ronald Foster, shouting into his microphone: "They just shot Harper! Be on the lookout for this car! — It is a Pontiac. It's got one tail light." Later on in the tapes, jurors listened as patrol cars were called to help in the impounding of a white Pontiac on the New Jersey Turnpike that the State claimed was the vehicle used by the killers of Trooper Werner Foerster. As the tapes were played, Assata was seated "calmly and without apparent concern" wearing a yellow turban and brightly colored floor-length dress over a white turtleneck sweater, according to news reports.

On February 23, Assata's attorneys filed papers asking Judge Appleby to subpoena FBI Director Clarence Kelley, Senator Frank Church, and other federal and New York law enforcement officials to testify about the Counter Intelligence Program (COINTELPRO), alleging it was designed to harass and disrupt black activist organizations. Kunstler had previously been successful in subpoenaing Kelley and Church for the trials of American Indian Movement (AIM) members charged with murdering FBI agents. The motion, which also asked the court to require the production of memos, tapes, documents, and photographs of alleged COINTELPRO involvement from 1970 to 1973, was denied.

For its first witness, on March 15 the defense called JoAnne Deborah Chesimard a.k.a. Assata Shakur; and her attorney, Stuart Ball, questioned her for under 40 minutes. She denied shooting either Harper or Foerster, and also denied handling a weapon during the incident. Ball's questioning ended with the following exchange:

(Stuart Ball)   "On that night of May 2nd, did you shoot, kill, execute or have anything to do with the death of Trooper Werner Foerster?"

(Assata Shakur) "No."

(Stuart Ball)   "Did you shoot or assault Trooper James Harper?"

(Assata Shakur) "No."

When she was cross-examined by prosecutor Edward Barone, she was unable to explain how three magazines of ammunition and 16 live shells had gotten into her shoulder bag. She admitted to knowing that Zayd Shakur carried a gun at times, and specifically to seeing a gun sticking out of Acoli's pocket while stopping for supper at a Howard Johnson's restaurant shortly before the shooting. She also admitted to carrying an identification card with the name "Justine Henderson" in her billfold the night of the shootout, but denied using any of the aliases on the long list that Barone proceeded to read.

Problems quickly developed within Shakur's defense team both in court and outside of court, Assata saying the reason being "too many cooks in the kitchen." Assata's attorneys, in particular Lennox Hinds, were often held in contempt of court, which the National

Conference of Black Lawyers cited as an example of systemic bias in the judicial system. Prior to becoming an attorney for Shakur, Hinds was also investigated by the New Jersey Legal Ethics Committee and faced possible disbarment for holding a press conference to denounce the trial of Assata Shakur as a "legalized lynching" by a "kangaroo court." Criticizing a trial while it was underway was a violation of the American Bar Association (ABA) rules. Judge Appleby also threatened Kunstler with dismissal and contempt of court after he delivered an October 21, 1976, speech at nearby Rutgers University that, in part, discussed the upcoming trial.

Evelyn Williams was faced with her own difficulties. Until eventually obtaining a court order, Williams was forced to strip naked and undergo a body search before each of her visits with Assata—during which Assata was shackled to a bed by both ankles.

As she had done in her previous trials, Assata Shakur constantly interrupted proceedings by yelling profanities, threatening the judge and jurors, and causing other disruptions throughout the nine-week court proceedings, although she would write years later in her autobiography that she "spent her time sitting there and looking up at the ceiling and hating herself for sitting there."

In order to put on a good defense, Shakur's legal team needed the testimony of a ballistics expert and a forensic chemist, among others, to refute the State's charges. They also needed an investigator to locate some of the doctors who had treated Assata while she was hospitalized, but funds were limited. Eventually, Judge Appleby issued an order that the State pay for the experts. However, this proved difficult since most of the experts the defense needed were either police or working with police agencies. Because the case involved the murder of a State Trooper, none of them would agree to testify, citing conflict of interest.

In August of 1976, Stanley Cohen suddenly died of unknown causes, although unsubstantiated reports state that he was physically attacked in his home. His offices and home had been searched, and it was determined from the items that were finally turned over to Williams and the remaining defense team by the authorities that at least half of the legal documents and other court papers related to Assata Shakur's case were missing. Shakur's lawyers also claimed that their offices were bugged. However, Judge Appleby decided not to order an investigation into the matter.

Following Cohen's death, tensions and dissension escalated among the remaining members of the defense team. Evelyn Williams felt that she was a victim of male prejudice and accused them of competing for center stage, while other members of the team were concerned that Williams was overly aggressive during her sole cross-examination to the point of passing her notes that read, in part, "You're antagonizing the jury" and "Shut up and sit down."

Sundiata Acoli, Assata Shakur, Trooper Harper, and a New Jersey Turnpike driver who saw part of the incident were the only surviving witnesses. Just as he did not testify in his own trial or give a statement to the police, Acoli did not testify or make any pre-trial statements in Shakur's trial. The driver traveling north on the turnpike at the time of the altercation testified that he had seen a State Trooper struggling with a black man between a white vehicle and a State Trooper car, whose revolving lights illuminated the area.

Assata testified that Trooper Harper shot her after she raised her arms to comply with his demand. She said that the second shot hit her in the back as she tried to avoid it, and that she fell onto the road for the duration of the gunfight before crawling into the backseat of the Pontiac—which Acoli then drove 5 miles down the road and parked. She testified that she remained there until State Troopers dragged her onto the road.

Trooper Harper's official reports state that after he stopped the Pontiac, he ordered Acoli to the back of the vehicle for Trooper Foerster—who had arrived on the scene—to examine his driver's license. The reports then state that after Acoli complied, and as Harper was looking inside the vehicle to examine the registration, Trooper Foerster yelled and held up an ammunition magazine as Shakur simultaneously reached into her red pocketbook, pulled out a nine millimeter weapon and fired at him. Trooper Harper's reports then state that he ran to the rear of his car and shot at Shakur who had exited the vehicle and was firing from a crouched position next to the vehicle.

Under cross-examination at both Acoli and Shakur's trials, Trooper Harper changed his testimony about Trooper Foerster yelling and showing him an ammunition magazine, about seeing Shakur holding a pocketbook or a gun inside the vehicle, and about Shakur shooting at him from outside the car. Retracting his previous statements, Trooper Harper said that he had never seen Shakur with a gun and that she did not shoot him.

In his testimony, Trooper Harper stated that when he first saw the Pontiac he was two miles north of the turnpike administration building, headquarters for the troopers. He followed the car for two miles until it was close to the administration building before he pulled it over because "the light was better and there was more security." He also stated during his testimony that the Pontiac was traveling at normal speed in the center lane. This statement would be contradicted by the testimony of Col. David B. Kelly of the New Jersey State Police who stated the car was traveling slightly over the speed limit.

Harper first passed the Pontiac in the left lane, observed the driver, and "made a mental note of his description," according to his testimony. He then moved to the right lane and let the Pontiac pass him, at which time he "made a mental note of the sex and race of the passengers." He then approached the Pontiac in the left lane, motioned the driver (Sundiata) to pull over, and called the administration building for assistance. When Trooper Robert Palentchar was directed to assist Harper, he commented over his radio, "Meet you at the pass, partner," although this was not picked up by dispatch. He then sped to the administration building at 120 miles an hour. Trooper Werner Foerster also went to assist in this "stop" for which, Harper testified, only a summons would have been issued.

In an article written by Assata Shakur's attorney Lennox Hinds and published by the *Covert Action Quarterly,* Hinds states:

Harper's testimony as well as that of all the other state's witnesses was riddled with inconsistencies and discrepancies. On three separate official reports, including his grand jury testimony, Harper said that he saw Assata take a gun from her pocketbook, while in the car, and shoot him. He admitted on cross-examination during both Sundiata's and Assata's trial, that he never saw Assata with a gun and did not see her shoot him - that, in fact, he lied.

A key element of Assata's defense was medical testimony meant to demonstrate that she was shot with her hands up and that she would have been subsequently unable to fire a weapon. Neurosurgeon Dr. Arthur Turner Davidson, Associate Professor of Surgery at Albert Einstein College of Medicine, testified that the wounds in her upper arms, armpit and chest, had severed the median nerve that instantly paralyzed her right arm, thus making it anatomically impossible for her to fire a weapon, would only have been caused if both arms were raised. Davidson based his testimony on an August 4, 1976, examination of Assata and on X-rays taken immediately after the shootout at Middlesex General Hospital.

Prosecutor Barone questioned whether Davidson was qualified to make such a judgment 39 months after the injury occurred, and then proceeded to recreate the scene while a female sheriff's attendant acted out his suggestion that Shakur was struck in the right arm and collar bone and "then spun around by the impact of the bullet so an immediate second shot entered the fleshy part of her upper left arm," to which Davidson replied, "Impossible."

Dr. David Spain, a pathologist from Brookdale Community College, testified that Assata's bullet scars as well as X-rays supported her claim that her arms were raised, and that there was "no conceivable way" the first bullet could have hit Shakur's clavicle if her arm was down.

Eventually, following the death of Stanley Cohen, Judge Appleby rescinded his order for the State to pay for the expert witnesses testifying on behalf of Assata Shakur, cutting off funds for any further expert defense testimony. Other evidence was presented, however. Neutron activation analysis administered after the shootout showed no gunpowder residue on Assata Shakur's fingers; and her fingerprints were not found on any weapon at the scene, according to forensic analysis performed at the Trenton, New Jersey, crime lab and the FBI crime labs in Washington, D.C.

Tape recordings and police reports made several hours after the shoot-out, when Harper returned on foot to the administration building 200 yards away, show he did not report that Trooper Foerster had been present at the scene, nor did Trooper Foerster notify dispatch of his whereabouts when he arrived at the scene. No one at headquarters knew of Foerster's involvement in the shootout until his body was discovered beside his patrol car, more than an hour later.

On March 24, the jurors listened for 45 minutes to a rereading of testimony of the New Jersey State Police chemist regarding the blood found at the scene, on the LeMans, and on Assata Shakur's clothing. That night, the second night of jury deliberation, the jury asked Judge Appleby to repeat his instructions regarding the four assault charges 30 minutes before retiring for the night. Appleby reiterated that the jury must consider separately the four assault charges (atrocious assault and battery, assault on a police officer acting in the line of duty, assault with a deadly weapon, and assault with intent to kill), each of which carried a total maximum penalty of 33 years in prison. The other charges were first-degree murder (of Foerster), second-degree murder (of Zayd Shakur), illegal possession of a weapon, and armed robbery (related to Foerster's service revolver). The jury also asked Judge Appleby to repeat the definitions of "intent" and "reasonable doubt."

CB BO

Photos

Assata addressing human rights
to Cuban delegation

Seabreeze Beach

Bobby Blue Bland

Manhattan Community College

NJ State Police Shield

NJ Turnpike Identification Sign

Trooper Werner Foerster

Eldridge Cleaver   Dhoruba-Bin-Wahad

Huey Newton and Bobby Seals
Black Panther Party

Mutulu Shakur

Mumia Abu-Jamal

Sundia Acoli

Zayd Malik Shakur

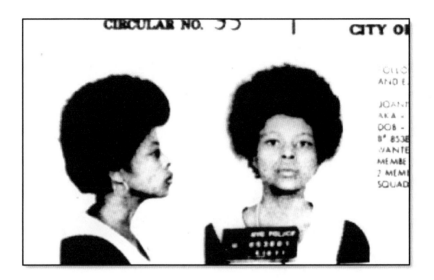

JoAnne Chesimard Wanted Poster

Assata Shakur During Trial

JoAnne Chesimard Exiting Court

J Edgar Hoover

Chokwe Lumumba

Evelyn Williams

Lennox Hinds

William Kunstler

Kamau Sadiki Fred Hilton

Judge - John E Bachman

Rikers Island

Edna-Mahan-Correctional-Facility-for-Women
(Formerly Clinton Correctional Facility)

Matteawan Hospital for the Criminally Insane

Marilyn Buck

Sister Mary Alice Chineworth

Sandra Good

Silvia Baraldini

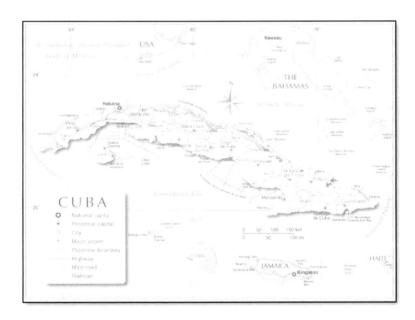

Assata Escaped to Cuba through the Bahamas

Assata Shakur in Cuba

Assata Shakur and her Daughter

Reward for information of her whereabouts leading to her apprehension
offered as two rewards, one of up to 1 million by the FBI
and the other of also 1 million offered by
the Attorney General of New Jersey.

Commercial Campaign "Assata Taught Me"

This mural of Assata Shakur was on display at the Marquette University
Gender and Sexuality Resource Center starting in March of 2015.
The mural was taken down one week later.

The William Morales/Assata Shakur room in CCUNY was changed to an annex for career services

Assata Shakur in Cuba

Cheri Laverne Dalton

Assata in Cuba – "Eyes of the Rainbow"

Middlesex County Memorial

Monument in Middlesex County
at the State Police Training Center in Edison

87

Fidel Castro – Retired President of Cuba.

US Embassy Reopens in Cuba, Aug 14, 2015

Raul Castro – President of Cuba

U.S. Department of State Continues to Request
Assata Shakur's Extradition

෨ ෬

Chapter Six

THE VERDICT

Assata Shakur was convicted on all eight counts: two murder charges, and six assault charges. The prosecution did not need to prove that Assata fired the shots that killed either Trooper Foerster or Zayd Shakur; being an accomplice to murder carries an equivalent life sentence under New Jersey law. After Joseph W. Lewis, the jury foreman, read the verdict, Kunstler asked that the jury be removed and then immediately sought a new trial on the grounds that one jury member, John McGovern, had violated the jury's sequestration order which Judge Appleby rejected. Afterwards, McGovern would sue Kunstler for defamation; Kunstler eventually publicly apologized to McGovern and paid him a small settlement. In his autobiography, Kunstler alleged that he later learned from a law enforcement agent that a New Jersey State Assembly member had addressed the jury at the hotel where they were sequestered, urging them to convict Shakur.

Upon hearing the verdict, Assata said—in a "barely audible voice"—that she was "ashamed that I have even taken part in this trial" and that the jury was "racist" and had "convicted a woman with her hands up." Judge Appleby told the court attendants to "remove the prisoner" and Assata replied, "The prisoner will walk away on her own feet." At the post trial press conference, Kunstler blamed the verdict on racism, stating that "the white element was there to destroy her (Assata Shakur)." When asked by a reporter that if that were the case, then why did it take the jury 24 hours to reach a verdict, Kunstler replied, "That was just a pretense." A few minutes later, prosecutor Barone addressed the reporters, disputing Kunstler's assessment and stating that the trial's outcome was decided "completely on the facts."

At the sentencing hearing on April 25, JoAnne Deborah Chesimard a.k.a. Assata Shakur sat handcuffed in the jury box as Judge Theodore Appleby of Superior Court sentenced her to 26 to 33 years in the state prison on the assault and weapons charges: 10 to 12 for the four counts of assault, 12 to 15 for robbery, 2 to 3 for armed robbery, plus 2 to 3 for aiding and abetting the murder of Trooper Foerster, to be served consecutively with her mandatory life sentence. However, Appleby dismissed the second-degree murder of Zayd Shakur, as the New Jersey Supreme Court had recently narrowed the application of the law. Appleby's final sentence was that Shakur serve 30 days in the Middlesex County Workhouse for contempt of court, concurrent with the other sentences, for refusing to rise when he entered the courtroom. To become eligible for parole, Assata would have had to serve a minimum of 25 years, which would have taken into consideration her four years in custody during the trials.

Due to the high security of the trial and the sequestration, Assata Shakur's trial, along with Acoli's, cost Middlesex County an estimated $1 million combined. In September 1977, New Jersey Governor Brendan Byrne vetoed a bill to give the Morris County sheriff $7,491 for overtime expenses incurred in guarding Shakur's jury.

After a bomb threat was made against Judge Appleby, Sheriff Joseph DeMarino refused to give the press the exact date of Assata's transfer to Clinton Correctional Facility for Women for security reasons. She was later transferred from the Clinton Correctional Facility for Women to a special area staffed by women guards at the Yardville Youth Correction and Reception Center in New Jersey, where she was the only female inmate. On May 6, 1977, Judge Clarkson Fisher, of the United States District Court for the State of New Jersey, denied Shakur's request for an injunction requiring her transfer from the all-male facility to Clinton Correctional Facility for Women; the Third Circuit affirmed.

In October 1977, New York State Superior Court Justice John Starkey dismissed murder and robbery charges against Assata Shakur related to the death of Richard Nelson during the December 28, 1972, hold-up of a Brooklyn social club, ruling that the State had delayed too long in bringing her to trial; "People have constitutional rights, and you can't shuffle them around."

The delay had been brought about as the result of an agreement between the governors of New York and New Jersey as to the priority of the various charges against Shakur. Three other defendants were indicted in relation to the same hold-up; Melvin Kearney, who died in 1976 from an eighth-floor fall while trying to escape from the Brooklyn House of Detention; Twymon Myers, who was killed by police while a fugitive; and Andrew Jackson, the charges against whom were dismissed when two prosecution witnesses could not identify him in a line-up.

On November 22, 1977, Assata pleaded not guilty to an attempted armed robbery indictment stemming from the 1971 incident at the Statler Hilton Hotel in which she was shot in the stomach. She was accused of attempting to rob a Michigan man staying at the hotel of $250 of cash and personal property, and was subsequently arrested, booked, and released on bail. The prosecutor was C. Richard Gibbons. The charges were dismissed without trial.

In 1978 Assata Shakur was transferred to Alderson Federal Prison Camp, a maximum security prison for women in Alderson, West Virginia, where she met Puerto Rican nationalist/activist Lolita Lebrón and Mary Alice Chineworth, former director of the Oblate Sisters of Providence, the nation's first order of black nuns. As a lifelong educator, activist, and seasoned leader, Sister Mary Alice introduced Assata to the concept of liberation theology, a Christian school of beliefs that developed in Latin America in the 1960s and 1970s, focusing on liberation of the oppressed.

While at Alderson, Assata ran into several members of the Aryan Sisterhood, a white supremacist prison gang, as well as Sandra Good, a follower of Charles Manson. Good had been indicted by a federal grand jury in Sacramento for "conspiracy to send threatening letters through the mail" in connection with death threats against more than 170 corporate executives who Good believed were polluting the earth. Also while at Alderson, Assata met Lynette "Squeaky" Fromme, another devotee of Charles Manson and would-be assassin best known for attempting to assassinate President Gerald Ford in 1975.

Because the Alderson Federal Prison Camp was being closed down, however, and other prisons considered her too great a security risk, Assata was shipped back to the New Jersey Corrections Institute for Women. A medium security prison, Assata Shakur and seven other women were housed in a separate, secure cell block for offenders considered high risks for violence or escape. "I was like Houdini," she would later claim in an interview for *Essence* magazine. "I plotted day and night. There was no way I was going to spend the rest of (my) life in prison for something I didn't do."

Throughout the pretrial and trial, Shakur's attorneys continued to argue that her conditions of confinement be improved, but to no avail. Lennox Hinds would state, Assata Shakur "understates the awfulness of the condition in which she was incarcerated," which included vaginal and anal searches. Assata claims that she was beaten and restrained by several large female officers after refusing a medical exam from a prison doctor shortly after giving birth. While imprisoned on Rikers Island, she filed a 42 U.S. Code § 1983 suit related to the conditions of her confinement. However, she was unsuccessful in persuading the federal courts to order that the legal aid paralegals assisting in her claim be granted attorney-like visitation rights.

Following the closing of the Maximum Security Unit at Alderson, Hinds argued, "In the history of New Jersey, no woman pretrial detainee or prisoner has ever been treated as she was, continuously confined in a men's prison, under twenty-four-hour surveillance of her most intimate functions, without intellectual sustenance, adequate medical attention, or exercise, and without the company of other women for all the years she was in custody."

As early as October 8, 1973, Angela Davis, a prominent counterculture activist and radical, as well as an April 3, 1977, *New York Times* advertisement purchased by the Eastern Coalition for Human Rights, identified Assata Shakur as a political prisoner. As reported in the October 26, 1998, issue of "Court Action Quarterly," on December 11, 1978, attorney Lennox Hinds, on behalf of the National Conference of Black Lawyers, the National Alliance Against Racism, and the Commission for Racial Justice of the United Church of Christ, sent a petition to the United Nations Commission on Human Rights alleging a "consistent pattern of gross ... violations of human rights and fundamental freedoms of certain classes of political prisoners in the United States because of their race, economic status, and political beliefs."

The petition, referring to the case of Assata Shakur, stated:

The FBI and the New York Police Departments, in particular, charged and accused Assata Shakur of participating in attacks on law enforcement personnel, and widely circulated such charges and accusations among police agencies and units. The FBI and the NYPD further charged her as being a leader of the Black Liberation Army, which the government and its respective agencies described as an organization engaged in the shooting of police officers. This description of the Black Liberation Army and the accusation of Assata Shakur's relation to it was widely circulated by government agents among police agencies and units. As a result of these activities by the government, Ms Shakur became a hunted person; posters in police precincts and banks described her as being involved in serious criminal activities; she was highlighted on the FBI's most wanted list; and to police at all levels she became a 'shoot to kill target.'

In response to the petition, seven international jurists representing the United Nations Commission on Human Rights visited a number of prisons on August 3-20, 1979, and reported their findings. They listed four categories of prisoners, the first of which were political prisoners, defined as "a class of victims of FBI misconduct through the COINTELPRO strategy and other forms of illegal government conduct who as political activists have been selectively targeted for provocation, false arrests, entrapment, fabrication of evidence, and spurious criminal prosecutions. This class is exemplified by: The Wilmington Ten, the Charlotte Three, Assata Shakur, Sundiata Acoli, Imari Obadele and other Republic of New Africa defendants, David Rice, Ed Poindexter, Elmer Geronimo Pratt, Richard Marshall, Russell Means, Ted Means, and other American Indian Movement defendants."

Even though Amnesty International did not regard Assata as a former political prisoner, the panel of jurists representing the United Nations Commission on Human Rights concluded in 1979 that Assata Shakur's treatment as a political prisoner was cruel and unusual punishment and "totally unbefitting any prisoner."

They also wrote in their report:

One of the worst cases is that of Assata Shakur, who spent over twenty months in solitary confinement in two separate men's prisons subject to conditions totally unbefitting any prisoner. Many more months were spent in solitary confinement in mixed or all-women's prisons. Presently, after protracted litigation, she is confined at Clinton Correctional Facility for Women in maximum security. She has never on any occasion been punished for any infraction of prison rules which might in any way justify such cruel or unusual punishment.

ༀ ༁

Chapter Seven

THE ESCAPE

On November 2, 1979, Black Solidarity Day, Assata Shakur escaped from the Clinton Correctional Facility for Women in New Jersey, and she immediately assumed the status of a folk hero. She likened herself to an escaped slave of the 20th century. It had been six years and six months to the day that she was arrested, two and a half years of which had been spent in solitary confinement. The day before, Assata had called her grandmother. Not knowing of her granddaughter's plan, her grandmother insisted that she "not get use to that place." The grandmother was prone to having dreams that more likely than not came true, and she had recently dreamed that her granddaughter was free.

Evelyn Williams learned from news reports that Assata Shakur had escaped from prison. Once again, her niece was a fugitive from the law. In New York, three days after her escape, thousands of demonstrators organized by the National Black Human Rights Coalition carried signs supporting her.

Leading up to the day of her escape, three men—two black, one white—requested visits with Assata Shakur four weeks in advance, as required by prison policy, but using bogus drivers' licenses and Social Security cards. However, prison officials never did the requisite background checks.

On the day of the escape, three members of the Black Liberation Army met in the waiting room at the prison entrance where they were processed through registration and shuttled in a van to the visiting room in South Hall. One of the men went ahead of the others. Although there was a sign stating that all visitors would be searched with a hand-held metal detector, he went through registration without being searched or patted down.

Meanwhile, the other two men were processed and neither was searched. As these two men were being let through the chain-link fences and locked metal doors at the visiting center, one of them drew a gun and took the guard hostage. Simultaneously, the man visiting Assata rushed the control booth, put two .45-caliber pistols to the glass wall, and ordered the officer to open the room's metal door. She obliged.

From there Assata Shakur and "the raiders," as they were called in several of the press reports, took a third guard hostage and, using the hostages as shields, they hustled Shakur outside to a prison van they commandeered earlier and where they had taken another hostage. Because only the maximum security section of the prison was fully fenced in, the van escaped through an unfenced section of the prison and across a grassy field into the parking lot of Hunterdon State School for the handicapped, 1.5 miles away, where two women were waiting to assist in the prison break in a blue-and-white Lincoln and a blue Mercury Cornet. No one was injured during the prison break, including the three guards held as hostages who were left in the parking lot.

Under questioning, State correction officials disclosed that they had not run identity checks on Assata Shakur's visitors or searched them, and that the three men who assisted in her escape had presented false identifications to enter the prison's visitor room.

Mutulu Shakur (born Jeral Wayne Williams), former Black Liberation Army member and resistance leader, Silvia Baraldini, active in both the Black Power and Puerto Rican independence movements and the driver of the second getaway car, former Black Panther Sekou Odinga (born Nathaniel Burns), and Marilyn Buck, an American Marxist revolutionary, were later charged with assisting in Assata's escape. Ronald Boyd Hill was also held on charges related to the escape.

Buck, said to be the only white member of the Black Liberation Army, and Assata Shakur, given the code name "Cleo" by her BLA handlers, allegedly hid out in Buck's East Orange, New Jersey, safe house before she was ferried to Buck's rented villa in the Bahamas. Attempts to locate Mutulu Shakur, whom Assata knew from her college days at Manhattan Community College when she was a member of the Republic of New Afrika, were unsuccessful.

Investigations conducted by the New York Joint Terrorist Task Force of the Federal Bureau of Investigation indicated that after the $1.6 million robbery of a Brinks armored truck in New York in which police officers Waverly Brown and Edward O'Grady and Brink's guard Peter Paige were murdered during the siege, and in which Mutulu was believed to have been involved, Mutulu Shakur had not returned to his New York home—an acupuncture clinic located at West 139th Street in Manhattan where, presumably, he also worked as an acupuncturist. He had been observed on several occasions entering an apartment in Greenwich Village, New York, but could not be located there after issuance of the arrest warrant.

Subsequent information led the FBI to Washington, D.C., where they discovered that Mutulu Shakur had rented an apartment under the fictitious name of "Donell Jackson." Coordinated efforts between the FBI and local authorities failed to locate Shakur at the apartment from when he had last been seen in Washington, D.C., in June 1982.

On July 23, 1982, the FBI placed Mutulu Shakur as the 380th addition on its list of "Ten Most Wanted Fugitives" where he remained for the next four years. Posters showing his photograph were circulated throughout the nation to federal and state law enforcement agencies, post offices, and the news media. He was eventually captured in 1986.

On November 24, 1982, while Mutulu Shakur remained at large, he and others were indicted in the Southern District of New York, of which Mutulu Shakur received eight counts of racketeering, corruption, three murders (two of which were murders of law enforcement officers), several armed robberies, and two armed kidnappings committed to effectuate the escape from prison of Black Liberation Army leader JoAnne Chesimard. In the aggregate, the charges against Mutulu Shakur carried a maximum prison sentence in excess of two life terms and a possible fine of $80,000.

Mutulu Shakur remained a fugitive throughout a five-month trial of his alleged co-conspirators during the spring and summer of 1983. A continuing investigation into the whereabouts of Mutulu Shakur and Cheri Dalton, another fugitive charged in the indictment, led the FBI to Los Angeles, California. There the FBI learned that Mutulu Shakur and Dalton had resided together under the fictitious names "David and Claudia Bryant" until May 1985, the month of the arrest of Marilyn Buck.

Mutulu Shakur's four-year evasion of the FBI came to an end on the morning of February 11, 1986, when he was arrested on a Los Angeles street by FBI Special Agent David Mitchell. At the time of his arrest, Mutulu Shakur was in possession of a California driver's license under the fictitious name of "Eugene Allen." The license listed a fictitious address and a fictitious date of birth as well.

Shortly after Mutulu Shakur's arrest, Agent Mitchell discovered a flyer entitled "BY ANY MEANS NECESSARY" in a public place in Los Angeles. The flyer purported to have been published by the "New Afrikan People's Organization." It was subtitled;

"STRUGGLE FOR THOSE

THAT STRUGGLE FOR YOU

MUTULU SHAKUR; FREEDOM FIGHTER,

NOT A TERRORIST"

The flyer asserted that "(t)he U.S. court system, in actual fact, has no moral or legal right to try Dr. Shakur .... We support Dr. Shakur being flown to a country where human rights are respected." The flyer concluded by urging fellow supporters to "Free Mutulu Shakur Now!"

On February 18, 1986, a magistrate in the Central District of California ordered Mutulu Shakur detained for trial on the grounds that he posed both a risk of flight and a danger to the community. Mutulu Shakur waived formal extradition proceedings and was transported in custody to the Southern District of New York where he was arraigned on the instant indictment on March 7, 1986. As he was led into the courtroom to be arraigned, Shakur announced to his supporters that he brought them greetings from "Nehanda," a name by which Cheri Dalton, still a fugitive, was known among Mutulu Shakur's supporters. After pleading not guilty to the charges in the indictment, Mutulu Shakur once again addressed his supporters:

I would like to first thank all of my supporters who have come out here today. Secondly, I wish to apologize for being caught. I am a New Afrikan Freedom Fighter.... As a captured freedom fighter of the New African Nation I am a prisoner of war. I demand to be treated in accordance with the Geneva Convention.

The most revealing evidence concerning the breakout of Assata Shakur came from admitted killer Tyrone Rison, who said he participated in the escape and, in a deal with prosecutors, testified in the Brink's trial of the two defendants, Mutulu Shakur and Marilyn Buck, in Federal District Court in Manhattan.

As the first witness to be called by the prosecution, Rison, 36 years old, began by identifying the defendants. He said Mr. Shakur had recruited him into the "family" in 1976, describing it as part of a revolutionary group that committed robberies to raise money for black liberation. When prosecutor Kerri Martin asked why the group had decided to arrange Ms. Chesimard's escape, Rison answered:

"We felt that just robbing Brink's trucks or guards or banks wasn't totally what we were about. It was time to do something that was totally political."

He was armed with an M-16, Rison told prosecutor Robert S. Litt during the Brinks trial, and he described how he had waited outside the prison in a van with Mutulu Shakur while Sekou Odinga had used a bogus identification card to enter the prison with a concealed revolver to give to Chesimard, who was called "Cleo." When Odinga and other members of the group brought Chesimard out, after holding three guards at gunpoint, they drove away in two cars, followed by the van. "We pulled off and went to a mall that was nearby the area," Rison said, adding that he and Mutulu Shakur then "got out of our van and went into a vehicle that was waiting to pick us up ... and we hid in the rear on the floor." They rode for about five minutes to "another vehicle that was waiting for us." The getaway cars were waiting at "switch points" and were driven by a "secondary team" from the group. "We got into the trunk of the vehicle that was waiting for us," he said, and they were taken to an apartment, or safe house, in East Orange, N.J.

The day after the prison breakout, Rison and Mutulu Shakur went to another safe house located in Mount Vernon, New York, where they took "a large sum" of cash from a safe "to give to Cleo" who was still at the East Orange apartment.

A month later in a Pittsburgh apartment Rison saw Chesimard with Odinga and other members of the group. It was there that Chesimard said she wanted to leave the country rather than stay in the United States. Libya, Angola, Cuba and China had been discussed as possibilities. It was decided that "we would help her leave the country" and that "she would leave through the Bahama Islands," Rison said. He then purchased plane tickets for a flight from Kennedy International Airport to the Bahamas, but had not gone on the trip himself, and he didn't know where she had gone after that. A week later Mutulu Shakur told him "the trip went smoothly."

In John Castellucci's book, *The Big Dance,* the author claims that eleven black and white radicals joined forces in the planning of

Assata Shakur's escape. In order to pay for weapons, lodging, and transportation, the group pulled off a $105,000 armored-car robbery two months before in Paramus, New Jersey.

Represented by Chokwe Lumumba, Mutulu Shakur maintained that he was a prisoner of war; as such, Lumumba sought pre-trial dismissal of the charges, claiming the acts charged against his client, Mutulu Shakur, were not criminal offenses but acts of war and resistance to genocidal oppression. Defendant Marilyn Buck joined the motion "as it applies to the conspiracy [charges in indictment 84 Cr.220 (CSG)] and as it applies to, in particular, the breakout of JoAnne Chesimard, also known as Assata Shakur." In a groundbreaking twenty-four page "Affidavit and Memorandum in Support of Motion to Dismiss the Indictment," Lumumba asserted, "The acts were committed in furtherance of the New Afrikan National liberation struggle in America," and "in pursuit of the objective of independence of the New Afrikan Nation from the United States."

Arguing before both the court and the press, Lumumba claimed Mutulu Shakur was implicated because of his "anti-colonial" activism, and he sought for his client the international protection afforded prisoners of war combating racist political regimes under Protocol 1 of the 1949 Geneva Convention, which had at that time been signed but not ratified by the United States. The Protocol classified "national liberation wars" as international conflicts, and afforded participants in such wars the same rights and protections as other soldiers. A national liberation war was defined as "any armed conflict" against a "colonial, racist or alien regime."

In his summary, Lumumba argued his client was covered by the Protocol, and the judge referred to the State Department the question whether the activities charged as a criminal enterprise against the defendants should be deemed an insurgency within the meaning of Protocol 1. The State Department responded that it did not recognize the Protocol, nor consider itself a party to a conflict with New Afrikan guerrillas.

Lumumba's immediate response was to the press: "Mutulu Shakur is a target ... because of his roots in the Black Liberation struggle. He is a target because of his affiliation with the Republic of New Africa and its link to the Prairie Fire Organizing Committee of the Weather Underground," referring to an activist group that believes all forms of oppression are created by the U.S. government and advocates its overthrow.

Lumumba's efforts failed. Mutulu Shakur was convicted on May 11, 1988. His first parole date was scheduled for December 15, 2016.

Marilyn Buck was one of the last suspects to be apprehended in the case. Her history with the Black Liberation Army dated as far back as 1973 when, at the age of 26, she was arrested for procuring firearms for the BLA and sentenced to 10 years in prison for buying two boxes of legal ammunition with a false ID. At the time, that was the longest sentence ever given for such an offense. In 1977 Buck was given a furlough from the federal women's prison in Alderson, West Virginia, where she first met Assata Shakur, but instead of returning at the designated time, she went underground.

Placed on the FBI's Most Wanted List and hunted with a shoot-to-kill order, Buck lived as a fugitive until 1985, when she was arrested outside a diner in Dobbs Ferry, New York, a little more than 10 miles from the site of an armored-car robbery in the Bronx for which she was also charged. A former private-school honor student, Buck drove one of the getaway cars the day that Assata Shakur escaped from prison. In the ensuing melee, she accidentally shot herself in the leg and was described in later years as walking with a noticeable limp.

In the following five years she faced four separate trials and was moved to three different jails and prisons. After two trials on lesser offenses, including an escape from prison charge, she along with several other defendants, together with Kathy Boudin, a prominent member of the Weather Underground, were convicted on several charges relating to the 1981 Brink's armored-car robbery in Rockland County, New York, in which three people were killed. She was sentenced to thirty years in prison. In 1988 she was tried and convicted, along with co-defendant Mutulu Shakur, of a RICO

(Racketeer Influenced and Corrupt Organizations) conspiracy to liberate Assata Shakur and commit several bank robberies—expropriations used to fund the Black Liberation struggle. Preparing for their trial, the two created legal arguments in their assertion of a political offense exception that remains today a model of how to pose the position of U.S. political prisoners in the context of international law. It is premised on the belief that individuals have the right to resort to political activism to foster political change.

On the same day in 1988 when sentence was pronounced in her RICO case, the government indicted Marilyn Buck, along with Alan Berkman, Linda Evans, Laura Whitehorn, Susan Rosenberg, and Tim Blunk, for what became known as the Resistance Conspiracy Case: "conspiracy to protest, oppose and change policies and practices of the U.S. government in domestic and international matters using violent and illegal means." The central charge in the case involved the 1983 bombing of the United States Capitol Building in response to the U.S. invasion of Grenada and shelling of Lebanon. Buck, Evans, and Whitehorn pleaded guilty in exchange for dropping the charges and getting better medical care for Alan Berkman, who was battling life-threatening lymphoma cancer. He died on June 5, 2009, at the age of 63.

The aggregate sentence from these cases was 80 years. Near the end of 1990 Buck began serving her sentence at the high security control unit for women in Marianna, Florida. Reflecting on this period, Buck later wrote:

The trials, those years of intense repression and U.S. government denunciations of my humanity had beat me up rather badly. Whatever my voice had been, it was left frayed. I could scarcely speak.

Nevertheless, while serving time in federal prison, Buck found a new outlet for her voice. She published numerous articles, poetry and essays, and other texts in journals and anthologies that received several honors from the PEN American Center's Prison Writing Program. Founded in 1971, the PEN American Center's Prison Writing Program provides one-on-one mentoring to inmates, conducts workshops, and seeks to promote inmates' work publicly through literary publications and readings. It is funded, in part, by the Stavros Niarchos Foundation, a leading international philanthropic organization which makes grants in the areas of arts and culture, education, health and medicine, and social welfare.

"For prisoners, writing is a life raft to save one from drowning in a prison swamp," Buck wrote. She also translated a volume of poetry, "State of Exile," by the Uruguayan writer Cristina Peri Rossi. Published in 2008 by City Lights Books, Rossi said of the collaboration in an interview with Latin Newspaper *El Tecolote*: "To learn how to turn suffering into something positive and creative is a necessary skill. I think this is a point Marilyn Buck and I share."

Buck also received a bachelor's degree in psychology from the New College of California in 1993, and a short time later, her Master of Fine Arts in Poetics. Buck was released from the Federal Medical Center, Carswell, on July 15, 2010, less than a month before her death at age 62 following a long battle with uterine cancer.

Sekou Odinga (born Nathaniel Burns), already a member of the Black Liberation Army underground for being a suspect in a police shooting, remained underground, partaking in revolutionary clandestine activity for twelve years until his capture. Upon being captured in 1981, he was charged with six counts of attempted murder, nine predicate acts of Racketeering Influenced Corrupt Organization (RICO), stemming from his alleged involvement in the escape of Assata Shakur from prison, and the $1.6 million Brink's armored car robbery in Nanuet, New York, involving BLA members and whites associated with the so-called Weather Underground.

At one point during the Brink's trial he was asked whether it was true that "the Black Liberation Army has taken credit for the assassination of police officers."

"Yes," Odinga said, "They've taken credit for that," justifying those actions as "retaliation for ongoing atrocities."

He was convicted in 1984 and sentenced to a consecutive twenty-five-years-to-life State sentence and a forty-year Federal sentence. Odinga was released from prison on November 25, 2014, after serving more than thirty years.

In 1982, Silvia Baraldini was sentenced to forty-three years under the Racketeer Influenced and Corrupt Organizations Act (RICO) for conspiring to commit two armed robberies, driving a secondary getaway car during the prison break of murder convict and fellow political activist Assata Shakur, and for contempt of court in refusing to testify before a grand jury that was investigating the activities of the Puerto Rican independence movement. Although the Black Liberation Army took responsibility for the bank robbery, Baraldini's attorney, Elizabeth Fink, argued that her client was neither accused nor convicted for any crime involving injury to another person. Nevertheless, the U.S. government sustained that her sentence was appropriate given the serious nature of her crimes.

Her supporters argued that her harsh sentence was due to her unpopular political beliefs, but her sentence held. Baraldini was imprisoned in numerous high-security facilities in the United States, including the notorious "control" unit in the basement of Federal Correctional Institution in Lexington, Kentucky, which housed two other women also convicted of politically motivated crimes; Susan Rosenberg, sentenced to 58 years in prison on the weapons and explosives charges, and Alejandrina Torres, sentenced to 35 years for seditious conspiracy. Both sentences were later commuted by President Bill Clinton in 1999. This special unit of 16 isolation cells was sharply criticized by Amnesty International and its closure was eventually ordered by U.S. District Judge Barrington Parker.

Also in 1999, during Bill Clinton's tenure as President of the United States, after five denials, the U.S. government agreed to a longstanding Italian request to allow political prisoner Silvia Baraldini to serve the remainder of her term in her native country. The move, announced by U.S. Ambassador to Italy Thomas Foglietta, appeared to be an attempt to appease Italian public opinion about the U.S. army plane that sliced a gondola cable when flying too low and too fast in the Italian Alps on February 3, 1998, killing twenty people. In that case, Italy returned the pilots involved in the *Strage del Cermis*

("Massacre at <u>Cermis</u>") tragedy, as it was called, and allowed them to be tried in their country of origin. The pilot, Marine Corps Captain Richard Asby, was acquitted by a U.S. military tribunal. Baraldini was transferred to Italy in order to serve the remainder of her sentence and was released on September 26, 2006, thanks to a pardon law approved in the previous months by the Italian Parliament.

In 1971, FBI Director J. Edgar Hoover announced that the centralized COINTELPRO was over and that all future counterintelligence operations would be handled on a case-by-case basis when the Citizens' Commission to Investigate the FBI burgled a two-man FBI field office in Media, Pennsylvania, took over 1000 classified documents, and exposed the program by passing this material anonymously to a number of news agencies. The theft resulted in the exposure of some of the FBI's most self-incriminating documents, including several detailing the FBI's use of postal workers, switchboard operators, and other resources, in order to spy on black college students and various non-violent black activist groups.

Using the Freedom of Information Act, which had been signed into law in 1966 by President Lyndon Johnson, to obtain documents from the government, NBC correspondent Carl Stern uncovered the long-running surveillance program known as COINTELPRO, and revealed what is now known as the infamous effort at political intimidation and disruption that may have been Hoover's biggest secret. Additional documents were revealed in the course of separate lawsuits filed against the FBI by a number of other groups and individuals that included the Socialist Workers Party (SWP) and the Young Socialist Alliance (YSA), and former UPS kingpin, the late Tom Forcade.

In 1976 the Select Committee to Study Governmental Operations with Respect to Intelligence Activities of the United States Senate, commonly referred to as the "Church Committee" for its chairman, Senator Frank Church, Democrat of Idaho, launched a major investigation of the FBI and COINTELPRO. The Final Report of the Select Committee addressed the violations of the intelligence community; and specifically, COINTELPRO:

The Committee finds that the domestic activities of the intelligence community at times violated specific statutory prohibitions and infringed the constitutional rights of American citizens. The legal questions involved in intelligence programs were often not considered. On other occasions, they were intentionally disregarded in the belief that because the programs served the 'national security' the law did not apply. While intelligence officers on occasion failed to disclose to their superiors' programs which were illegal or of questionable legality, the Committee finds that the most serious breaches of duty were those of senior officials, who were responsible for controlling intelligence activities and generally failed to assure compliance with the law. Many of the techniques used would be intolerable in a democratic society even if all of the targets had been involved in violent activity, but COINTELPRO went far beyond that ... the Bureau conducted a sophisticated vigilante operation aimed squarely at preventing the exercise of First Amendment rights of speech and association, on the theory that preventing the growth of dangerous groups and the propagation of dangerous ideas would protect the national security and deter violence.

At the time of Assata Shakur's escape in 1979, lead defense attorney, William Kunstler, had just started to prepare her appeal. Following her escape, Assata lived as a fugitive for several years. The FBI circulated wanted posters throughout the New York/New Jersey area while, in response, her supporters hung anonymously-printed bright yellow posters on signposts throughout Harlem with Assata's photo and the message, "Assata Is Welcome Here."

For years after Assata Shakur's escape, the phone calls, movements, and activities of her friends and relatives—including her daughter walking to school in upper Manhattan—were monitored by investigators in an attempt to ascertain her whereabouts. In July 1980, FBI Director William Webster said that the search for Assata Shakur had been frustrated by residents' refusal to cooperate, and a *New York*

Times editorial suggested that the department's commitment to "enforce the law with vigor—but also with sensitivity for civil rights and civil liberties" had been "clouded" by an "apparently crude sweep" through a Harlem building in search of Shakur. In particular, one pre-dawn April 20, 1980, raid on 92 Morningside Avenue was seen by residents as having "racist overtones" when, according to the residents, fifty police officers and FBI agents armed with shotguns and machine guns broke down doors and searched through the building for several hours, while preventing residents from leaving.

Other published reports stated that the New Jersey and New York City Police had declined to raid places where Assata Shakur was suspected to be hiding in fear of provoking a racial incident. In October, 1981, dozens of Nassau County and Garden City police officers showed up to arrest a 23-year-old female wall cleaner when a tipster mistakenly reported her as being Assata Shakur.

"Cleo," with the help of her supporters, managed to elude the FBI for five years by vanishing underground.

 C3 &0

... I was put in a unit with about 15 members of the Aryan Sisterhood which is the sister organization of the Aryan Brotherhood, which is a neo-Nazi organization and famous for 'torching'. 'Torching' means, in prison language, throwing lighter fluid or some other inflammable substance into a cell, and then throwing a match. Who they are famous for torching are black prisoners. So I became convinced that the prison authorities were trying to kill me while I was in prison.

When she was later moved to the Clinton prison in New Jersey, prison officials immediately placed severe restrictions on the other women in her area, something that created an atmosphere of anger and hatred toward her and the constant threat of assault from her inmates.

Once she was granted asylum in Cuba, she was given a government-paid two-story stucco house on 90th Street in Havana's fashionable Playa section not far from a cluster of foreign embassies. The walls of the book-cluttered, modestly furnished one-bedroom home were covered with paintings by Cuban artists. The Cuban government paid approximately $13 a day toward her living expenses as well as her rent that was less than $50 a month, according to Shakur.

Assata Shakur's generous treatment from the Cuban government isn't unusual. Through the years, other fugitives deemed to be genuine revolutionaries also have received ration cards and free housing from the Castro regime, as well as college educations and cushy jobs. Some have worked at propaganda stations beaming revolutionary rhetoric at the United States. Others have taught English at elite Havana schools.

In 1968, Black Panther William Lee Brent, a former bodyguard for leader Eldridge Cleaver, hijacked a passenger plane, TWA Flight 154, to Cuba after shooting two San Francisco policemen. The Castro government, fearing he was a spy for the United States, immediately confined him to an immigration jail in Havana where he spent the next 22 months at hard labor, primarily working in the sugar cane fields. After his release, however, Brent earned a Spanish literature degree from the University of Havana and taught English at junior and senior high schools. He also sometimes met with visiting foreigners and journalists, and served as a Cuban emissary to the left-wing government of Grenada during the 1980s, even though he never became a Cuban citizen. Brent recently died of bronchial pneumonia and is buried in an unmarked grave in the pauper's portion of *Cementerio de Cristóbal Colón* (Colón Cemetery) in the Vedado neighborhood of Havana, where eight coffins are stacked atop one another and then topped with concrete. Brent, who was 75 at the time of his death, holds position No. 5.

One large Havana home became known as the "Hijack House" because so many of its occupants arrived on pirated aircraft. Neighbors referred to another as *Casa de las Panteras* (Panther's House) because of all the fugitive Black Panthers living there.

Black Panther chief Eldridge Cleaver—who fled to Cuba after a shootout with Oakland police—lived in a penthouse which came with the services of a personal maid and cook and stocked with all the food, rum, and cigars he would need at the courtesy of the Castro regime. In addition, he received on loan from the Cuban government several AK-47 rifles for hunting expeditions. However, when Fidel learned that the CIA had infiltrated the Black Panther Party, he no longer trusted Cleaver and withdrew his Cuban hospitality. After a disagreement between Castro and Cleaver that involved a tense standoff of several weeks during which time Cleaver reminded Castro that he still had the AK-47 rifles, they arrived at a mutual agreement that Cleaver would move on to Algeria. Eldridge Cleaver set up an international office for the Black Panthers while in Algeria, but an incessant long-distance feud between Cleaver and Huey Newton resulted with the international branch's expulsion from the party in 1971.

Following the split, Cleaver along with his wife, Kathleen, and their allies formed a new organization, the short-lived Revolutionary People's Communication Network. Its stated reasons for formation were: "to replace the former Ministry of Information of the Black Panther Party; to provide a new structure for dissemination of information and mass organization in keeping with the new conditions of struggle; and to structurally and organizationally separate the above-ground and underground apparatus of the revolutionary forces fighting inside the United States."

For a while Cleaver lived in France where he underwent a religious experience before returning to the United States as a born-again Christian and, later, a Reaganite, declaring that "the American political system is the freest and most democratic in the world." Cleaver's charges from the shoot-out in 1968 were eventually reduced to assault and he was sentenced to community service. Although he never admitted it, there are some who believe Cleaver worked for either the CIA or FBI undercover in exchange for a reduced sentence. Suffering from heavy cocaine addiction, Cleaver died in Pomona, California, on May 1, 1998, at the age of 62.

As recently as the 1990s, the FBI had a list of 91 fugitives from terrorist-type charges living in Cuba. But researcher Latner believes there are no more than two dozen left, perhaps only half that. Still, they include some big names: Ishmael LaBeet, one of five men convicted of the infamous Fountain Valley Massacre, a racially-tinged 1972 armed robbery in St. Croix, Virgin Islands, that turned into mass murder, with eight dead; William Morales, the master bomb-maker of the Puerto Rican separatist group FALN, which set off 140 or so blasts around the United States during the 1970s and 1980s, killing at least six people; Victor Gerena, an armed robber working for another Puerto Rican separatist group, who is believed to have taken the proceeds of a $7 million heist to Cuba with him.

The biggest name of all remains Assata Shakur.

Today, an eight-foot-high chain-link fence with a green tarpaulin hides the house on the other side where Assata Shakur used to live, blocking the view of passers-by, and featuring an elaborate lock on the main gate and driveway. The current resident says that Shakur moved out years ago and did not leave a forwarding address.

When first arriving in Cuba in the early 1980s, Assata lived openly, working as a part-time teacher, seminar leader, translator,

English-language editor for Radio Havana Cuba, author, and mentor in Havana's black community. She also served as a hostess for delegations of international visitors. "I'm invited to give lots of presentations to people who come here. I talk about human-rights' violations and political prisoners in the United States," she told *Essence* magazine, although she has "tried as much as possible to avoid the standard 9-5 thing."

Occasionally she met with members of Havana's fledgling hip hop artists. Popular in the mid-1990s, it started across the bay from Havana in Regla, Cuba, a poor community with a provincial character that was home to freed slaves, as a social protest movement by Afro-Cubans against what they saw as a racist society. Today, the rhyme isn't so much about the Castro brothers or politics, but about the black experience, machismo, sexism, and inequality.

The first few years of exile provided the time Assata needed to focus on more creative outlets. "I'm still very active in political work," she told Evelyn White of *Essence* magazine in the 1990s. "I'm putting finishing touches on another book. I talk about gender relations, rap music, crime and so forth, in a question-and-answer format. I ask my own question and then answer myself, so the book is a bit shizy. But it's the form that I thought would best get across the points I want to make."

When asked what life was like in Cuba, she was quick to answer:

It's been good. It was hard at the beginning because I had to adjust to another culture and learn another language. I had to adjust to living in a Third World country, which means that things people in the U.S. take for granted—like hot running water whenever you turn on the tap—are not always available here. But it's been a growing and happy experience for me in many ways. Another thing I've been able to do in Cuba is rest. You live such an intense life in the States. And my life has been more intense than most. Being in Cuba has allowed me to live in a society that is not at war with itself. There is a sense of community. It's a given in Cuba that, if you fall down, the person next to you is going to help you get up.

She went on to describe how she spends her time each day:

I run. I live here on an island surrounded by all this water and I'm a lousy swimmer. It's pitiful. I've started to crochet again, which is something I learned in prison. I'm going to be a grandmother soon, so with the crochet, I can make gifts for my daughter and the baby. I'm totally into this grandmother thing. I'm starting to paint and write fiction. I'm in a more creative stage of life. There's something about approaching 50 that's very liberating. Political struggle has always been a 24-hour-a-day job for me. I felt I could never take time out for myself. Now I feel I owe it to myself to develop in ways I've been putting off all my life. I'm crafting a vision of my life that involves creativity. And Cuban society allows me to do this. I know it's harder in the U.S. where so many people are just grateful to have a job.

In another interview by *The Talking Drum* she was asked if the Africanness of Cuba provided solace, to which Assata replied:

The first thing that was comforting was the politics ... So living here was an affirmation of myself, it was like 'Okay, there are lots of people who get outraged at injustice.' The African culture I discovered later. At first I was learning the politics, about socialism – what it feels like to live in a country where everything is owned by the people, where health care and medicine are free. Then I started to learn about the Afro-Cuban religions, the Santeria, Palo Monte, the Abakua. I wanted to understand the ceremonies and the philosophy.

Over the years of living in exile, Assata has been vocal about other differences she has found in Cuba as compared to the United States, especially between the blacks in Cuba and the blacks in the United States. Some of these differences she writes about in an open letter—From Exile with Love:

My life wasn't beautiful and creative before I became politically active. My life was totally changed when I began to struggle ... But that's what it means to be Black in the Americas, a life of struggle. Blacks in Cuba and the United States share a history of slavery yet their paths separate in how they view their lives ...

117

We've (Blacks in America) forgotten where we came from. People in Cuba have not lost their memory. They don't suffer from historical and cultural amnesia. Cuba has less material wealth than America but are able to do so much with so little because they know where they come from ... This was a maroon country. The maroons escaped from slavery and started their own community. Everyone needs to identify with their own history. If they know their history, they can construct their future ... The Cubans identify with those who fought against slavery. They don't identify with the slave master. Those who made the revolution won't let the people forget what happened to them. The people here seriously study history ... We have to de-Eurocentrize the history we learn. We have to give the real perspective of what happened. We have to create a world to know and remember our own ... We believe we're free but we're not. Our world vision is tainted ... We are oppressed people in the U.S. and don't even know it ... Our problem is that we want to belong to a society that wants to oppress us. We want to be the plantation owner. In Cuba, we want to change the plantation to a collective farm.

Until as recently as 2014, Assata freely gave interviews to visiting American journalists. She was easy to find; her name and telephone number were listed in the Havana phone directory. She easily blended into the population and lived in the community with the rest of the Cubans. However, that has now changed. Many believe that Castro was upset by too many interviews in which she complained about living conditions in Havana, and that she has taken on a new identity, or she's living under the direct control and support of the government in some elite enclave in order to avoid the risk of having her wandering around on the streets.

Like some seventy other fugitives from American justice, Assata Shakur lives in Cuba at the whim of Castro, and is facing increasing pressure from the United States to extradite her. Now with the recent turn of events between the governments of the United States and Cuba, and the opening of trade and travel regulations toward the restoration of diplomatic relations, friends of Assata say she fears she will be returned to a New Jersey prison cell to finish serving a life sentence.

In addition, she worries that she might be kidnapped by ordinary Cubans seeking the $2 million bounty offered by the New Jersey State Police and the FBI for her capture. "In terms of what she's doing, who she sees—I have no idea," said Cheri Laverne Dalton, a fellow Havana-based fugitive from American justice who was linked to Shakur's prison escape. In a 2015 interview by *The Record*, Dalton explained: "She has become intensely secretive now about her comings and goings in Havana, and only her closest confidants know her exact address and phone number."

Other associates say that since the reward for her apprehension is so high, she moves from place to place on the island, under the protection of Cuban security. Once a star attraction on the Cuban government's cultural reception circuit, she has virtually disappeared in recent times.

New Jersey Governor Chris Christie, U.S. Senators Ted Cruz of Texas and Marco Rubio of Florida, along with Senator Bob Menendez of New Jersey and others, have demanded that Assata Shakur be returned to prison in the United States. However, the White House declined to say whether Assata's status—and that of other Cuba-based U.S. fugitives—would be part of any talks with Cuba, now or in the future. For the time being, Cuban officials, citing Assata's guarantee of political asylum from Fidel Castro himself, insist that she and the others will not be a factor in any negotiations with the United States.

Assata Shakur's U.S. attorney, Lennox Hinds, a professor of criminal justice at Rutgers University, stated to *The Record:* "Obviously, there is a manhunt for her. There are private bounty hunters who are out there in addition to the official government intelligence agencies ... It is a very serious security issue. And it's a matter of life and death for her." He also added that whenever he travels to Cuba, he is monitored.

There have been several other acquaintances interviewed in recent months, and when asked about Assata, they all agree that she is living in fear. One American official who was based in Havana said he once stuck a wanted poster into her fence, just to let her know that her case was not forgotten. The woman now living in the house where Assata lived when first arriving in Cuba says, "I think she wanted to be alone," as to explain why she moved.

Cheri Laverne Dalton, who still goes by the name Nehanda Abiodun and refers to herself as a rap music activist, revealed that the last time Assata had called her, the two of them discussed their grandbabies. Referring to the reward set up in 2013 by the FBI and the State of New Jersey, "You know she has $2 million on her head," Dalton said, adding that Assata "has to be extremely cautious."

Dalton fled to Cuba in the mid-1980s after she was accused of participating in Assata Shakur's prison escape. She was also indicted by federal authorities for allegedly helping leftist militants, including members of the BLA and the Weather Underground, steal $1.6 million from a Brinks armored truck at the Nanuet Mall in Rockland County in October 1981. Two Nyack police officers were killed along with a Brinks security guard. It was almost a decade later in testimony during the trial of one of the Brinks' robbers that Dalton was first linked to Shakur's escape.

Dalton has a $100,000 bounty for her capture and is listed as a "domestic terrorist" on the website of the FBIs New York field office, which is overseeing her investigation. In the interview with *The Record,* she declined to discuss her alleged role in Assata Shakur's escape from the Clinton Correctional Facility—now the Edna Mahan Correctional Facility for Women.

In December 2014, *The New York Post* interviewed several Cubans living and working in Havana and ironically, few interviewed even knew Chesimard was in the country—and those who did had no knowledge of the $2 million reward posted by the New Jersey State Police and the FBI. Several admitted that they would turn her over without thought for the reward. "A Cuban would sell out his mother for that kind of money. Money is what talks," declared Carlos, a Havana merchant who was interviewed. "A Cuban will sell you out for 5 pesos. Imagine $2 million," added Juan, a hotel worker in the capital.

More recently, *14ymedio,* the first independent digital media outlet in Cuba, published an article on the ramifications of extraditing JoAnne Chesimard aka Assata Shakur to the United States in view of the new relations between the two countries. Founded on May 21, 2014, by the Cuban blogger and activist <u>Yoani Sánchez</u> and the Cuban journalist Reinaldo Escobar, the newspaper contains news about Cuba and the world in topics related to national politics, international politics, economy, culture, society, science and technology, and sports. It also publishes editorials, opinion articles, and interviews.

Located in one of the countries with the lowest internet connectivity across the globe where the government controls all media and regularly blocks access to websites that are hostile to its administration, the newspaper operates without access to the internet and uploads the information by using Wi-Fi access from hotels.

Given the government control of the media in Cuba, most of the people leaving comments did so anonymously. These comments were translated into English from Spanish and Cuban Spanish, a form of Caribbean Spanish or Lucumí, a dialect of the West African language Yoruba that includes French and indigenous Taino. They all basically agree that the Cuban Adjustment Act—a U.S. federal law to adjust the status of Cuban refugees to that of lawful permanent residents of the United States after certain criteria are met—will soon become irrelevant. In addition, several offer opinions on what should be done with JoAnne Chesimard aka Assata Shakur:

The Cuban government has always had a foreign policy based on political blackmail. I see why they do not want to deliver the dark-haired killer, who is not even a relevant political figure and has no money ... the sole reason the Cuban government protects the dark lady (JoAnne Chesimard) without receiving anything in return is for an exchange, not for money but for nothing more and nothing less than Posada Carriles. You ever seen such impudence ... The man was acquitted of their charges also is a U.S. citizen which is why it makes no sense to have this exchange. What it is... is an old grudge that Fidel has with Carriles, and Castro wants to see Carriles killed before Castro dies. They have already made several attempts and one of them left him almost dead ... As for me let Cuba keep the blackie ... anyhow, here the jails and the streets are full of them....

***

The talks should focus on the real criminals and demand that the bad government by those who are in power in Cuba finish installing things like internet, empower the self-employed, and to stop repressing dissent.

***

I think the military dictatorship based in Havana should extend an "invitation" to Assata Shakur to be a resident in another country... If her presence in Cuba is becoming uncomfortable for the dictatorship, something that already is being felt, and she represents an economic advantage for the dictatorship out of it, they will trade her...

***

If the gringos make it a good deal to Raul, the Blackie is (expletive).

***

That black woman is a killer, lethal injection.

***

I do not understand. This woman is not Snowden whose head is worth a lot of money but did not kill anyone. It would be understandable in the case of Snowden for its political importance but this woman is a common delinquent, not only killed the police at point-blank but was convicted to life in prison by a court with all the rights and then escaped from a federal prison and came to Cuba saying she was a civil rights activist. It is true that the woman was a Member of the Black Panthers but of a subgroup that were terrorists who used bombs and robbed banks etc.

***

Nobody wants to know about this gangster - she does not even have any money and is not worth a halved penny and goes wandering through the streets of Havana with impunity. How many criminal acts has this murderer committed in the decades of living in Cuba probably living off the charity figures like Jessie Jackson and Danny Glover. Finish this - just deliver this woman who does not agree to anything with the new policy between the two countries....

Both the FBI and the New Jersey State Police continue to monitor Assata Shakur's activities in Havana, although they don't say how, and sources at both agencies confirm that Assata has assumed a much lower profile in the years after the bounty for her capture was announced and then doubled. Special Agent Celeste Danzi, a spokeswoman for the FBIs Newark Field office which is leading the Shakur investigation, says, "JoAnne Chesimard continues to remain a fugitive wanted by the FBI. She is a domestic terrorist. She murdered a law enforcement officer. Until she is brought to justice to serve her sentence, we will continue to keep her on the wanted list."

Terrence Jennings, a New York-based photographer who specializes in portraits of hip hop artists, told reporter Mike Kelly that he saw Assata on a Havana street a few years ago. At first reluctant, Assata then joined Jennings at a café, and during their conversation she discussed the 1973 gun battle on the New Jersey Turnpike in which Foerster was shot and killed, execution style, with his own gun. "She said she was acting in self-defense," Jennings said.

Cuban hip hop artist, Soandry Del Rio, said in an interview with *The Record* that he often wondered how the African-American woman, who braided her shoulder-length hair and who sometimes talked about racism back home in America, could ever truly adjust to Cuba. In the last few years, Del Rio said, she often seemed skittish and fearful of coming to any meeting if she was not familiar with everyone who attended. This came to be seen by many in the hip hop community as part of Assata Shakur's personality. "She looked like somebody who accepted her own destiny," Del Rio said. "But I think that she was not happy here."

৪০ ০৪

Chapter Nine

AFTERMATH

Assata Shakur was interviewed on television in February of 1998 showing her as a vibrant, articulate grandmother and author at age 50. During the interview, Assata discussed how she regularly addresses religious and human rights delegations in Cuba. Following the interview, New Jersey Governor Christine Todd Whitman announced that she would intensify her crusade to extradite or "kidnap" Shakur from her 14-year exile in Cuba, and that she would send her State Attorney General Peter Verniero to hand deliver a letter to U.S. Attorney General Janet Reno demanding that the federal government facilitate whatever ways or means it takes to return Shakur from Havana to face life imprisonment in the United States. (Assata Shakur in Cuba is an) "affront to law enforcement and our system of justice," Governor Whitman said. In addition, Governor Whitman allocated $50,000 as a reward for Assata Shakur, and lobbied federal officials for help in bringing her back.

Senator Robert G. Torricelli lent support by applauding the passage of House Resolution 254, which calls on Cuba to return Assata Shakur. He wrote to Castro, urging him to return her because her "brutal actions left behind a grieving widow, and a son forced to live the remainder of his life without his father."

On May 2, 2013, FBI Special Agent Aaron Ford from the Newark field office announced that 65-year-old fugitive JoAnne Chesimard a.k.a. Assata Shakur had been named to the list of Most Wanted Terrorists—the first woman to make the list of top terrorists and joining ranks with warlords of the Palestinian Islamic Jihad and Saudi Hezbollah masterminds. In his statement, Special Agent Ford said, "While living openly and freely in Cuba, she continues to maintain and promote her terrorist ideology. She provides anti-U.S.-government speeches, espousing the Black Liberation Army's message of revolution and terrorism."

In addition, the State of New Jersey matched the bounty of $1 million on her head offered by the FBI, thereby replacing the original bounty set by New Jersey Governor Christine Todd Whitman of $50,000, and bringing the total to $2 million. Under President Barack Obama and Attorney General Eric Holder, the announcement was designed to commemorate the 40th anniversary of the New Jersey Turnpike shooting. "I hope that they can get her," Trooper Foerster's widow, Rosa, 72, said from her home in Florida. "She's still there. She has her freedom, and I don't have my husband. That's what's hard about it." Ms. Chesimard was named to the list because she is "a supreme terror against the government," Agent Ford said at the news conference. Chesimard, a 65-year-old grandmother at the time of the announcement, along with being the first woman on the list, is the second domestic terrorist after Daniel Andreas San Diego, a straight edge vegan and animal liberationist who has an alleged association with the Animal Liberation Brigade cell responsible for bombing two biotechnology and nutritional products corporations in 2003.

As part of a media blitz that includes alerts on the traditional outlets of television, radio and the internet, the FBI has tapped into a huge pool of potential tipsters, the tens of thousands of motorists plying major highways in the Northeast. The FBI's digital billboard program, a partnership with Clear Channel and other national outdoor advertising companies that donate the ad space, began as a one-city test in Philadelphia in 2007 and expanded to twenty cities the following year. It now comprises a network of several thousand locations throughout the country.

Access to the towering electronic boards gives the FBI a valuable tool in its crime-fighting arsenal, and "we reach a wider audience," said FBI Special Agent Barbara Woodruff, a spokeswoman for the Newark field office. "We have access to these billboards in times of extreme importance, to include national emergencies, fugitive-related cases and kidnappings. Some people don't always read the paper (and) newspapers don't always pick up press releases," she added. "Millions of people commute every day, and they're staring at the billboards."

The FBI's Newark Division tapped into the New Jersey network of electronic billboards on May 2, 2013, to mark the 40th anniversary of the execution-style slaying of state trooper Werner Foerster on the New Jersey Turnpike in 1973. This time it was to publicize the doubling to $2 million of the reward for information "leading to the capture of JoAnne Chesimard, the Black Liberation Army member who was convicted of murdering New Jersey State Trooper Foerster and one of its Most Wanted Terrorists." Posters featuring the FBI's 10 Most Wanted fugitives are now regularly cycled into the advertisement rotation on digital billboards from coast to coast.

On December 23, 2014, Josefina Vidal, Cuba's foreign ministry head of North American affairs, told the Associated Press that the communist nation would not return Shakur despite public requests to do so from New Jersey Governor Chris Christie and acting State Attorney General John Hoffman. Both Christie's and Hoffman's requests came after President Obama announced the restoration of full diplomatic relations with Cuba for the first time in 54 years. "We've explained to the U.S. government in the past that there are some people living in Cuba to whom Cuba has legitimately granted political asylum," Vidal said. "There's no extradition treaty in effect between Cuba and the U.S."

In December 2015, when President Obama announced a new era of thawed relations with Cuba, after more than fifty years of isolation, Assata Shakur's case regained the national spotlight, with several top conservatives, including New Jersey Governor Chris Christie and New Jersey Senator Robert Menendez, calling for Cuba to hand her over. They and other officials have asked for Shakur's return to be a requirement of renewed diplomatic ties between the two countries. In a letter to Secretary of State John Kerry, Menendez said that Cuba's refusal to return the now 69-year-old Shakur "is an intolerable insult to all those who long to see justice served."

Even after all this time, Assata Shakur continues to be a vocal activist, speaking out on such issues as global justice and the prison industrial complex, and influencing other black nationalism agendas and movements. A lot of her rhetoric still advocates "armed struggle"—insisting that blacks must use "armed struggle" as one of many approaches in their quest for a better life in the United States.

In July 1973 she wrote "To My People" while in prison, stating in part:

My name is Assata Shakur (slave name joanne chesimard), and i am a revolutionary. A Black revolutionary. By that i mean that i have declared war on all forces that have raped our women, castrated our men, and kept our babies empty-bellied.

I have declared war on the rich who prosper on our poverty, the politicians who lie to us with smiling faces, and all the mindless, heart-less robots who protect them and their property.

I am a Black revolutionary, and, as such, i am a victim of all the wrath, hatred, and slander that amerika is capable of. Like all other Black revolutionaries, amerika is trying to lynch me.

She concludes her letter by rallying "her people" with these words:

It is our duty to fight for our freedom.

It is our duty to win.

We must love each other and support each other.

We have nothing to lose but our chains.

In "A Message to My Sistas," written in 2005, she seems to advocate that all black women rise up and take full responsibility for the black race:

At this time, I'd like to say a few words especially to my sisters:

SISTERS. BLACK PEOPLE WILL NEVER BE FREE UNLESS BLACK WOMEN PARTICIPATE IN EVERY ASPECT OF OUR STRUGGLE, ON EVERY LEVEL OF OUR STRUGGLE. I think that Black women, more than anybody on the face of the earth, recognize the urgency of our situation. Because it is We who come face to face daily with the institutions of our oppression. And because it is We who have borne the major responsibility of raising our children. And it is We who have to deal with the welfare systems that do not care about the welfare of our children. And it is We who have to deal with the school systems that do not educate our children. It is We who have to deal with the racist teachers who teach our children to hate themselves. It is We who have seen the terrible effects of racism on our children.

As she celebrated her 60th birthday in 2007, she wrote:

In some ways it was easier for my generation. Racism was blatant and obvious. The "Whites Only" signs let us know clearly, what we were up against. Not much has changed, but the system of lies and tricknology is much more sophisticated. Today young people have to be highly informed and acutely analytical, or they will be swept up into a whirlpool of lies and deception.

129

Freedom, justice and liberty are words that are thrown around a lot in the United States, but for most of us, it is empty rhetoric. With each and every passing day the country becomes more repressive, the police more viciously aggressive and the so-called constitutional guarantees obliterated by scare tactics. The so-called 'Conservatives' are only interested in conserving their privileges and power and helping their rich friends to become richer. Black 'Conservatives' serve their "masters" and are basically interested in grinning, shuffling and 'Uncle Tomming' all the way to the bank. This is the most corrupt administration that has ever existed.

In 1987, Lawrence Hill & Company in the United States and Canada published *Assata: An Autobiography,* which was written by Shakur in Cuba. Angela Davis and Lennox Hinds both wrote forewords to the book in which Assata refers to herself in the lower case "i". In the six months prior to the publication of the book, Evelyn Williams, Shakur's aunt and attorney, made several trips to Cuba and served as a go-between with Hill. Because of the "Son of Sam" laws which restrict who can receive profits from a book, the copyright is held by Zed Books Ltd. of London, and in 2014, they released a revised edition. In her book, Shakur does not give any details of the events on the New Jersey Turnpike other than to say that the jury "convicted a woman with her hands up!"

In 1993, Shakur published a second book, *Still Black, Still Strong,* with Dhoruba bin Wahad and Mumia Abu-Jamal, which is described as "an essential document of the Black Panther Party written by three leading thinkers and party activists who were jailed following the FBI'S 1969 mandate to destroy the organization 'by any means possible.'"

In an open letter dating back at least to 1998, Shakur addressed the public, stating:

Black people, poor people in the U.S. have no real freedom of speech, no real freedom of expression and very little freedom of the press. The black press and the progressive media has historically played an essential role in the struggle for social justice. We need to continue and to expand that tradition... I feel that people need to be educated as to what is going on, and to understand the connection between the news media and the instruments of repression in Amerika. All I have is my voice, my spirit and the will to tell the truth.

Assata Shakur's voice continues to be heard not only in her books and letters, but in the legal and educational institutions across the country, as well as in the news and entertainment media.

In institutions of higher learning, her name and writings have found both a place of influence and disagreement. Following a storm of controversy brought on by an April 4, 1995, editorial in the *New York Post*, based on an item the paper said it saw in a small West Coast periodical called *Heterodoxy*, the Borough of Manhattan Community College renamed a scholarship that had previously been named for Shakur. Over the years, fifty students studying at the Borough of Manhattan Community College where Assata first attended in 1967, prior to joining the Black Liberation Army, had received $500 scholarships named for the Communist North Vietnamese leader, Ho Chi Minh, and for JoAnne Chesimard, "the convicted murderer of a New Jersey police officer."

At Bucknell University, taught by James Peterson, an assistant professor of English, in 2008 Assata was featured in a course on "Black Heroes"—along with figures such as Harriet Tubman, Sojourner Truth, John Henry, Malcolm X, and Angela Davis.

And Assata's autobiography, together with those of Angela Davis and Elaine Brown, the only women activists of the Black Power movement who have published book-length autobiographies, is excerpted in a class on "Crime and Punishment in American Literature," taught by Professor H. Bruce Franklin, at Rutgers University.

On December 12, 2006, Matthew Goldstein, the Chancellor of the City University of New York, directed City College's president, Gregory H. Williams, to remove the "unauthorized and inappropriate" designation of the "Guillermo Morales/Assata Shakur Community and Student Center," when an article appeared in *The*

Daily News stating that CUNY was honoring terrorists. The center had been named by students in 1989 when a student protest group won the right to use the lounge after a campus shutdown over proposed tuition increases. As a result, on October 22, 2013, officials at City College of the City University of New York under the direction of Chancellor William Kelly shut down the Guillermo Morales/Assata Shakur Student and Community Center, turning Room 3/201, the small physical space that was the center for student activism, into an annex for career services at the college, the *New York Times* reported. All the Morales-Shakur Center's belongings were moved out and apparently placed into storage, and the room and exterior doors, which were once red with a black fist, were painted white.

While the center was much loved by some activist groups, it had been criticized for years by others. Guillermo Morales, a Puerto Rican nationalist revolutionary accused of planting bombs for the Armed Forces of National Liberation (FALN), and Assata Shakur were both City College alumni who fled from the United States to Cuba. City College officials said that the closing was based on space needs, not politics. But students organized protests, calling the move an attempt to squelch student activism in "the only liberated space in CUNY."

In 2015, New Jersey's Kean University rescinded its invitation to have hip hop artist Common speak at the event after members of the State Troopers Fraternal Association of New Jersey voiced their anger over Common's A track on the singer's 2000 album Like Water for Chocolate entitled "A Song for Assata," on which Cee Lo Green proclaims of the tune's heroine, "Your power, your pride is beautiful."

The Gender and Sexuality Resource Center at Marquette University celebrated the completion of a mural featuring convicted Assata Shakur in May 2005. A short time later, the director of the center, Susannah Bartlow, was terminated and the mural was removed. The mural, which was the joint project of the Center and the

Alpha Kappa Alpha sorority, displayed the stylized portrait of Assata Shakur and two of her quotes:

No one is going to give you the education you need to overthrow them. Nobody is going to teach you your true history, teach you your true heroes if they know that that knowledge will help set you free.

Before going back to college, I knew I didn't want to be an intellectual, spending my life in books and libraries without knowing what the hell is going on in the streets. Theory without practice is just as incomplete as practice without history. The two have to go together.

Other organizations, various media, and entertainers have stepped up to advance Assata Shakur's cause. In 1997, Assata appeared in a 47-minute documentary, "Eyes of the Rainbow." The official premier of the film in Havana in 2004 was promoted by *Casa de las Américas*, the main cultural forum of the Cuban government. Written and directed by Cuban filmmaker Gloria Rolando, it deals with Assata's life, her history, and living in Cuba, told in the context of Assata's Afro-Cuban connections, including the Yoruba Orisha Oya, goddess of the ancestors, of war, of the cemetery and of the rainbow, from which the title of the documentary is taken. In the film, Shakur emphatically and passionately declares, "I am a prisoner … I have always been a prisoner" in reference to African slaves being forcibly brought to the United States and from which she descended. She also discusses one of her favorite topics—her views on the failings of the penal system in the United States:

Prisons are big business in the United States, and the building, running and supplying of prisons has become the fastest-growing industry in the country. Factories are moving into the prisons, and prisoners are forced to work for slave wages. This super-exploitation of human beings has meant the institutionalization of a new form of slavery. Those who cannot find work on the streets are forced to work in prison.

In response to the $2 million reward offered for the capture of JoAnne Deborah Chesimard aka Assata Shakur, the National Conference of Black Lawyers (NCBL), formed in 1968 to serve as the Black Liberation movement's legal arm and aid other black activists, issued a statement demanding "that the U.S. government immediately withdraw the bounty offer, and permanently cease its pursuit of Assata Shakur as such is both illegal and unjustifiable under international human rights laws"... and, as such, "NCBL takes the ongoing attacks on Assata Shakur personally." Assata's long-time attorney, Lennox Hinds, served for many years as National Director of the National Conference of Black Lawyers of the United States and Canada.

In 2005, several leaders and supporters of the New Black Panther Party protested in front of the Earle Cabell Federal Courts Building in downtown Dallas, Texas, during the afternoon to show their displeasure with the United States government and how it labels Shakur as a terrorist.

On July 1 of that same year, the *Millions for Assata* (Philadelphia) *Campaign* was initiated by Sister Kathleen Cleaver (widow of Eldridge Cleaver), Sister Empress Phile' Chionesu (originator and president of Million Woman March/Movement), Sister Pam Africa (longtime member of the Black Nationalist group MOVE), Sister Rosemari Mealy (Black Panther member and activist in the international human rights and political prisoner movement), and others "in order to bring greater attention and awareness to the continual COINTELPRO, Patriot Act, and outright racist capitalistic acts and attempts initiated directly upon Sister Assata Shakur, and indirectly on the sovereign country of Cuba." It is the stated goal of the *Millions for Assata* to "further galvanize supporters, worldwide, to hold rallies, demonstrations, and to sign on to the petition to have the million-dollar bounty that has been placed on Assata's head revoked."

On March 10, 2012, in Newark, the New Black Panther Party rallied *In Defense of Assata*. "We are pathetically living in an era where the U.S. government's foreign policy is crippling the world with its doctrine of 'Regime Change,'" explained an angry Zayid

Muhammad, a longtime friend and supporter of Assata and organizer of the rally.

The *Hands off Assata Campaign*, as defined on the www.assatashakur.org website, "is a coming together of organizations and individuals who are outraged by the heightened attempts by the federal government, congress of the united states and the state of new jersey to illegally force thru kidnapping a return of Assata Shakur from Cuba to the plantation United States." In addition, the *Hands off Assata Campaign Action Alerts* "use networks of ordinary citizens from all over the world to educate, agitate and compel change."

A *Hands off Assata* rally, organized by the New Black Panther Party, was held on May 10, 2013, in Newark. The New Black Panther Party for Self-Defense (NBPP) is a U.S.-based black political organization founded in Dallas, Texas, in 1989. Despite its name, NBPP is not an official successor of the Black Panther Party. Members of the original Black Panther Party have insisted that the newer party is illegitimate and have firmly declared, "There is no new Black Panther Party."

Also, as an acknowledgment of support for Assata Shakur, described as a "day of celebration and education on the liberation of Assata Shakur," on November 2, 2013, the *Assata Liberation Day Celebration* was held at the University of the District of Columbia, School of Law, in Washington, DC.

Within the entertainment field, in 2005 American hip hop recording artists, entrepreneurs, and social activists Mos Def and Talib Kweli got together at City Hall in New York City with R&B singer/musician Martin Luther and City Councilman Charles Barron to demand that the federal government drop the $1 million bounty on Shakur's head and remove her from the domestic terrorist watch list.

Lonnie Rashid Lynn Jr., better known as the hip hop artist-Chicago rapper, Common, who recorded "A Song for Assata" as a tribute to her after traveling to Havana to meet with Shakur personally, came under the spotlight glare once again when protests erupted over his participation in a White House PG-rated poetry slam for school children, at the invitation of Michelle Obama. Common, sitting on a stool and wearing a light-gray suit, rapped in a quiet rhythmic verse of young people who suffer and die in a society hobbled by poverty and retribution:

Destiny's children — survivors, soldiers — in front of buildings their eyes look older.

It's hard to see blessings in a violent culture.

Former Deputy Chief of Staff and Senior Advisor to President George W. Bush, Karl Rove decried the recording artist and film star as a "thug" and "misogynist," while Sarah Palin, the former Governor of Alaska and GOP Vice Presidential nominee took to Facebook with a sardonic, "Just lovely, White House." Fox News called the rapper "vile," as the labor union representing New Jersey State Troopers voiced robust opposition. Meanwhile, Obama press secretary Jay Carney found himself struggling to debate the nuances of hip hop with the media corps over Common's usual rap lyrics, such as:

the black strap to make the cops run

when I go/ I want to be known like El-Hajj Malik El-Shabazz.

And,

I don't know what it is/ but white girls gettin' ass/ I know what it is/ It's cash.

Digable Planets, Paris ("Assata's Song"), 2Pac, Digital Underground, The Roots, Asian Dub Foundation, Saul Williams, Rebel Diaz, Murs, Jay Z, Public Enemy, and X-Clan have recorded similar songs about Shakur. Due to her support in the rap and hip hop community, Assata Shakur has been alternately termed a "rap music legend" or a "minor cause celebre."

In the second season of television series *Madam Secretary*, there is an episode in which an Assata-like character, played by L. Scott Caldwell, is approached by the Secretary of State, played by

Téa Leoni, and acknowledges that she had been wrongly convicted. The issue is resolved by promising to provide the support of the State Department to the Assata character in a new trial in the U.S.

The *BlackLivesMatter* movement began in 2013 with the use of the hashtag #BlackLivesMatter on social media after the acquittal of George Zimmerman in the shooting death of African-American teen Trayvon Martin. It soon became internationally recognized for its street demonstrations following the 2014 deaths of two African Americans, Michael Brown, resulting in protests and unrest in Ferguson, and Eric Garner in New York City. Today, *BlackLivesMatter*—the activist group that demands a "racial justice agenda" that includes constant criticism and activism against police— invokes the words of convicted cop killer Assata Shakur at "all its events." Co-founder Alicia Garza writes:

When I use Assata's powerful demand in my organizing work, I always begin by sharing where it comes from, sharing about Assata's significance to the Black Liberation Movement, what its political purpose and message is, and why it's important in our context.

At a recent event for female bloggers, *BlackLivesMatter* leaders had a crowd of thousands repeating lines from a letter written by Shakur that include an explicit reference to the Communist Manifesto: "You have nothing to lose but your chains!"

In April 2016, while speaking at a town hall event in the Royal Horticultural Halls of central London, President Obama took the opportunity to offer a measured criticism of the *BlackLivesMatter* movement:

I think that what BlackLivesMatter is doing now to bring attention to the problem of a criminal justice system that sometimes is not treating people fairly based on race, or reacting to shootings of individuals by police officers has been really effective in bringing attention to problems.

But he also advised young people to seek compromises and to work within the system:

One of the things I caution young people about though, that I don't think is effective, is you've highlighted an issue and brought it to people's attention ... and elected officials are ready to sit down with you, then you can't just keep yelling at them. And you can't refuse to meet because that would compromise the purity of your position.

Also in February, the Public Broadcasting Station aired the documentary, "The Black Panther Party: Vanguard of the Revolution," as part of its Independent Lens series. In the documentary, African-American director Stanley Nelson combines R&B songs from the 1960s and 1970s, interviews with FBI agents and former Panthers, and archival footage showing the Panthers' trademark natural Afro hair styles, dark glasses and black leather jackets that were so popular during that time.

It is the latest in a long list of feature films and documentaries about the Oakland group that shook the establishment then—and continues to cause controversy even today. Right wingers claim the film ignores criminal and thuggish behavior by the group. Others criticize the film for not digging deep enough into black liberation history.

Other support groups include *Assata Taught Me*, a commercial campaign to sell tee shirts and hoodies with the slogan that is to replace "Hands up, don't shoot." And out of Chicago comes the black activist intergenerational group, *Assata's Daughters*, named in her honor. Claiming to be inspired by the "Radical Monarchs," *Assata's Daughters* states, "We aim to support young Black women's leadership and participation within the *Black Lives Matter* movement: Unapologetically Black, young, radical women."

The government and law enforcement, as well as other interested parties, haven't given up either. William Callahan, a corporate intelligence consultant and President of Unitel, reveals that in 1989 he was approached by a group in Texas to "snatch JoAnne Chesimard out of Cuba." He describes the incident as follows:

Castro didn't give a damn who she (JoAnne Chesimard) was or what she did; all that mattered was he wanted to punch the USA in the eye. There was a sizable cash bonus offered to me so I went to Miami and met with a Cuban emigre who laid out his plan. After I studied it for a few days, I realized there were too many holes in the plan and passed on it. The risk factors were too great—using a fishing trawler to come within 25 miles of the coast at night and then a hi-speed small boat to take three heavily-armed specialists onto a beach where he was guaranteeing she would be bound and lying there waiting for the pick-up.

In 1997, Carl Williams, the superintendent of the New Jersey State Police, wrote a letter to Pope John Paul II asking him to raise the issue of Assata Shakur's extradition during his talks with President Fidel Castro. "It's a long shot, but we figured we could ask," said state police spokesman Al Della Fave. "At least it would be a way to get the ear of Fidel."

While the pope was in Cuba in 1998, Assata Shakur agreed to be interviewed by NBC journalist Ralph Penza. Shakur later published an extensive criticism of the NBC segment, which inter-spliced footage of Trooper Foerster's grieving widow with an FBI photo of Assata connected to a bank robbery of which she had been acquitted. In part, Shakur stated:

In January of 1998, during the pope's visit to Cuba, I agreed to do an interview with NBC journalist Ralph Penza around my letter to the Pope, about my experiences in New Jersey court system, and about the changes I saw in the United States and it's (sic) treatment of Black people in the last 25 years. I agreed to do this interview because I saw this secret letter to the Pope as a vicious, vulgar, publicity maneuver on the part of the New Jersey State Police, and as a cynical attempt to manipulate Pope John Paul II... After years of being victimized by the "establishment" media it was naive of me to hope that I might finally get the opportunity to tell "my side of the story." Instead of an interview with me, what took place was a "staged media event" in three parts, full of distortions, inaccuracies and outright lies.

Penza, who died in 2007, also interviewed Col. Williams in the same story who stated the FBI had a detective working full time on tracking "Chesimard," and that "Chesimard better be looking over her shoulder all the time."

In response to the FBI's letter written to Pope John Paul II, in 1998, *Democracy Now!* aired Shakur's reading of her own 1874-word letter to the pope, during his trip to Cuba, in which she discusses her situation while stating that she is not writing to ask that he intercede on her behalf:

In 1977 I was convicted in a trial that can only be described as a legal lynching. In 1979 I was able to escape with the aid of some of my fellow comrades. I saw this as a necessary step, not only because I was innocent of the charges against me, but because I knew that [in] the racist legal system in the United States I would receive no justice. I was also afraid that I would be murdered in prison. I later arrived in Cuba where I am currently living in exile as a political refugee.

In her letter, she claims to have been targeted by COINTELPRO and as a result:

I have advocated and still advocate revolutionary changes in the structure and in the principles that govern the U.S. I advocate an end to capitalist exploitation, the abolition of racist policies, the eradication of sexism, and the elimination of political repression.

She specifically denounces the State of New Jersey, stating:

The New Jersey State Police are infamous for their racism and brutallty. Many legal actions have been filed against them and just recently, in a class action legal proceeding, the New Jersey State Police were found guilty of having an "officially sanctioned, de facto policy of targeting minorities for investigation and arrest."

Couched in an admission of her own faith …

… All my life I have been a spiritual person. I first learned of the struggle and the sacrifice of Jesus in the segregated churches of

140

the South. I converted to Catholicism as a young girl. In my adult life I have become a student of religion and have studied Christianity, Islam, Asian religions and the African religions of my ancestors. I have come to believe that God is universal in nature although called different names and with different faces ...

... she addresses other grievances that include problems within the prison system, human rights violations, racism, and drugs. The letter was recorded and printed in publications around the world.

Meanwhile, the FBI has continued with its attempts to recapture Assata Shakur. In 1999, the FBI requested the assistance of Kamau Sadiki, the father of Assata Shakur's daughter, Kakuya Amala Olugbala, in a collaborative effort to recapture Shakur, a political exile living in Cuba. When Sadiki did not comply, based on new evidence, the Atlanta police re-opened the 1971 case where Atlanta Police Officer James Green was murdered.

In 2001, a former BLA member gave a statement about the 1971 murder, linking Sadiki, after being detained during a traffic stop. With no eyewitness testimony and no physical evidence, the State based its case entirely upon the statements of three former BLA members who were present in Atlanta at the time of Officer Green's murder.

Sadiki was arrested in 2002 in Brooklyn, New York, some thirty-one years later after the murder and found guilty by a Fulton County Superior Court jury. On November 10, 2003, Judge Stephanie Manis sentenced Kamau Sadiki to life imprisonment for murder and ten (10) years to run consecutively for armed robbery. Kamau Sadiki, #0001150688, continues to serve his sentence at the Augusta State Medical Prison where he suffers from hepatitis C, cirrhosis of the liver, and sarcoidosis, a disease that leads to inflammation of the body's organs.

Sundiata Acoli, Assata's co-defendant in the New Jersey Turnpike trial, after being found guilty for the murder of Trooper Foerster and sentenced to life in prison in the New Jersey State Prison, remained in the Management Control Unit (MCU) created for him and other politically associated prisoners for almost five years. In September 1979, the International Jurist interviewed Sundiata Acoli and subsequently declared him a political prisoner. A few days later, prison officials secretly transferred him during the middle of the night to the federal prison system at Marion, Illinois. Court records show that Acoli was captured while trying to escape in 1982, and in July 1987 he was transferred to the federal penitentiary at Leavenworth, Kansas.

He received 27 disciplinary citations in prison between 1974 and 1996, which his attorney, Bruce Afran, argued "were minor" when he came up for parole in 1994. For the 1994 parole hearing, Acoli was not permitted to appear before the New Jersey Parole Board in person and was only allowed to participate from USP Leavenworth via telephone without an attorney present. After a 20-minute telephone hearing Acoli was denied parole. In 2004, once again there was the possibility for parole, but he did not get it. Then, on September 29, 2014, a New Jersey state appeals court officially granted Acoli's request for parole, finding that the panel had ignored evidence in Acoli's favor. Court records revealed that a psychologist testified in 2010 that Acoli had "expressed regret and remorse about his involvement" in the killing and was at "low to moderate risk" of re-offending. The appellate panel ordered the board to "expeditiously set conditions for parole."

However, the State of New Jersey appealed this ruling, and "the decision is now in the hands of the state Parole Board," said Lee Moore, a spokesman for the state Attorney General's Office. "The statute provides for a full Parole Board hearing with the benefit of input from, among other individuals, Trooper Werner Foerster's surviving loved ones," Moore said.

The Supreme Court said the Appellate Court acted prematurely because a person convicted of first-degree murder would have to be ordered released by the full 15-member Parole Board. In this case, the full board only affirmed that a two-member panel hadn't made errors in denying Acoli's parole bid. "That process in its totality requires a full hearing before the Parole Board on his suitability for parole release and shall permit the victims of Acoli's criminal acts to be heard, if they wish, by the board prior to a decision on his parole," said the court, in February 2016, in a 4-1 majority opinion written by Justice Jaynee LaVecchia.

Chris Burgos, president of the State Troopers Fraternal Association, also criticized the Appellate Court's ruling. "We do not believe arguments that a person convicted of the murder of a law enforcement officer and conspiring the violent overthrow of the U.S. government can be rehabilitated, or considered to have paid their debt to society in full," Burgos said in a statement.

According to court records, Acoli told a state psychologist in 2010 that he was no longer associated with Black Nationalists' groups and was eager to return home to his daughters. While he has apologized for his role in Foerster's murder, Acoli has claimed he was grazed by a bullet and blacked out during the shootout, and couldn't remember the exact sequence of events. Col. Rick Fuentes, who spoke at the dedication of a monument in Foerster's memory, said there was no evidence Acoli had been grazed by a bullet and that he presented a high risk to the public if released. "I don't see him as really changing his stripes over the years—his feelings, his ideology and politics, or his attitude toward law enforcement," Fuentes said. "He may say he's remorseful and apologize for his role, but then he hides his role."

Acoli's attorney contended his client had reformed, adding that he was "confident" the board would approve parole because of his clean prison record. "Today Sundiata Acoli, 79 years old, is one of the most praised and model inmates in the federal prison system," Afran said. "He is as far removed from the person he was in 1973 as possible."

Acoli is now waiting to appear before the Parole Board for a full hearing before he is eligible for release.

In the meantime, others who are closely connected to Assata Shakur have attempted to escape the drama that continues to cloud her life.

Kakuya Amala Olugbala Shakur, Assata's daughter who is now 42 years old, returned to the United States and lived for a time in Chicago, Illinois. It is believed that she has since relocated to the northeast where her son, Che, is receiving medical care courtesy of the American people.

Evelyn Williams, Assata's aunt, attempted to move on with her life and continue her career as an attorney. However, her defense of her niece had made her a target of harassment for years, and she eventually lost her private legal practice. From 1987 to 1989 Williams taught at City College of New York, then entered private practice again with the New York City law firm of Stevens, Hinds and White, where she continued to work for social change for the African American community. Now semiretired, she admits that she has reached the same conclusion that her niece reached a long time ago; "Direct action by the people is the only hope for change."

Before her death in 1995, Assata's mother, Doris, endured the hardships and anguish brought on by the actions of her daughter by such things as the phone ringing constantly in the middle of the night with an unknown caller telling her that her daughter was dead.

CB BO

Chapter Ten

EXTRADITION

On March 19, 1998, New Jersey Governor Christine Todd Whitman asked Attorney General Janet Reno to do whatever it takes to return Shakur from Cuba. Later that same year, U.S. media widely reported claims that the United States State Department had offered to lift the Cuban embargo in exchange for the return of 90 U.S. fugitives, including Assata Shakur.

Also in 1998, the United States Congress passed a non-binding resolution asking Cuba for the return of Shakur as well as 90 fugitives believed by Congress to be residing in Cuba; House Concurrent Resolution 254 passed 371-0 in the House and by unanimous consent in the Senate, due in no small part to the lobbying efforts of Governor Whitman and New Jersey Representative Bob Franks. Prior to the passage of the Resolution, Franks stated: "This escaped murderer now lives a comfortable life in Cuba and has launched a public relations campaign in which she attempts to portray herself as an innocent victim rather than a cold-blooded murderer."

Senator Robert G. Torricelli lent support by applauding the passage of House Resolution 254, which calls on Cuba to return Assata Shakur. He wrote to President Raúl Castro, urging him to return her because her "brutal actions left behind a grieving widow, and a son forced to live the remainder of his life without his father."

As a result, Shakur's supporters were spurred to create the "Hands off Assata" campaign as a platform to voice their outrage. Largely internet-based, it is coordinated by Chicago-area Black Radical Congress activists and organized by Dream Hampton for the purpose of "support(ing) the international human rights and Geneva conventions, which enabled her (Assata Shakur) to seek and secure political asylum in Cuba, and we support the right of the Cuban people to grant it to her."

In addition, Congressional Black Caucus Representative Maxine Waters of California wrote an open letter to Castro explaining that many members of the Caucus, including herself, were against Shakur's extradition, and called COINTELPRO an "illegal, clandestine political persecution."

The National Conference of Black Lawyers (NCBL) continues to remain vocal, adamantly stating:

Assata Shakur's failure to find justice within the U.S. system compels NCBL to analyze her circumstances according to international law standards. The Universal Declaration of Human Rights provides in various of its Articles that everyone is entitled to: freedom from arbitrary arrest, detention and exile; freedom from torture, and cruel and inhuman or degrading treatment; the right to a presumption of innocence at trial; and the right to seek and to enjoy in other countries asylum from persecution. Assata Shakur has been flagrantly and continuously denied each of these rights and others by a U.S. government that, as Shakur herself has observed, is hell bent on making an example of her in much the same way slave owners of an earlier era hunted down runaway Africans, and returned them to the plantation for purposes of public torture.

NCBL will direct inquiries to officials involved in this matter, and otherwise begin an investigation into the facts and circumstances that led to these events. NCBL will, according to its obligation to the African World, make public all of its findings.

In a television address, prior to Fidel Castro's transfer of presidential duties to his brother Raúl in 2011, Castro called Assata Shakur a victim of racial persecution, according to the Associated Press, saying "they (the U.S. government) wanted to portray her as a terrorist, something that was an injustice, a brutality, an infamous lie."

In 2013, the FBI announced it had made Shakur the first woman on its list of most wanted terrorists. The reward for her capture and return was also doubled to $2 million that year. Shakur's profile on the FBI website shows a list of 23 aliases, the FBIs account of her conviction and escape, two birthdates, and an explanation that Shakur "may wear her hair in a variety of styles and dress in African tribal clothing. She is one of only two American-born people listed, the only woman, and the only person of African descent.

Angela Davis, American political activist, academic scholar, and author, has said, "It seems to me that the attack on (Assata Shakur) reflects the logic of terrorism, because it precisely is designed to frighten young people, especially today, who would be involved in the kind of radical activism that might lead to change."

In December 2014, President Obama ordered the restoration of full diplomatic relations with Cuba and the opening of an embassy in Havana for the first time in more than a half-century as he vowed to "cut loose the shackles of the past" and sweep aside one of the last vestiges of the Cold War. The surprise announcement came at the end of 18 months of secret talks that produced a prisoner swap negotiated with the help of Pope Francis and concluded by a telephone call between President Obama and President Raúl Castro.

Immediately after the president's announcement, the New Jersey State Police issued a statement saying the move to normalize relations with Cuba presents an opportunity to bring Shakur back to finish her sentence in Foerster's murder. "We stand by the reward money and hope that the total of two million dollars will prompt fresh information in the light of this altered international relationship." The State's acting Attorney General John Hoffman said his office would be working with federal authorities to find a way to "return her to her rightful place in a New Jersey prison."

Jeff Rathke, a spokesman for the State Department, said the decision to drop Cuba from the state sponsor of terrorism list it has occupied since 1982 "reflects our assessment that Cuba meets the statutory criteria. While the United States has significant concerns and disagreements with a wide range of Cuba's policies and actions, these fall outside the criteria relevant to the rescission of a state-sponsor-of-terrorism designation," Rathke said.

The U.S. Attorney General's office did not respond to questions about whether it urged the administration to seek her extradition in its negotiations with Cuba—or whether it would push for it now. Bernadette Meehan, National Security Council spokesperson, would not address the Shakur case directly, but she said the U.S. "will continue to press for the return of U.S. fugitives in Cuba to pursue justice for the victims of their crimes in our engagement with the Cuban government."

It is unclear exactly how many U.S. fugitives live in Cuba at this time, but Teishan Latner estimates the number to be less than 40. Latner has done extensive research and writing on the role Shakur has played in U.S.-Cuba relations. More than any other political exile in Cuba, he says, Shakur "grew to symbolize Cuba's provision of sanctuary to American dissidents." She embodies "both the FBI's campaign to retrieve fugitives from the island and the Castro government's commitment to sanctuary even in the face of strong diplomatic pressure."

On April 11, 2015, Presidents Barack Obama and Raúl Castro shook hands at the Summit of the Americas in Panama, marking the first meeting between a U.S. and Cuban head of state since the two countries severed their ties in 1961. The meeting came four months after the presidents announced their two countries would restore diplomatic relations, and gave rise to President Obama's March 2016 visit to Cuba, the first by a sitting president in over eighty-five years.

Just prior to the meeting between Presidents Obama and Castro, Col. Rick Fuentes, superintendent of the New Jersey State Police, wrote an "opinion" piece for the *New York Post*, stating in part his concerns for the safety of American tourists planning to travel to Cuba where terrorists continue to live openly:

President Obama is going to Cuba next week, the first official state visit by a sitting president in more than 80 years ... It'll surely be followed by regularly scheduled domestic airline and cruise-ship service, rock concerts, major sporting events, US corporate investment and thousands of American tourists curious to see Marxism up close and how an entire country can be reduced to an underclass.

Havana is where most of the tourists will likely travel ... But Americans, beware ... You also should know that some of America's most wanted terrorists are living openly in Cuba. These still-dangerous revolutionaries roam the island, disenchanted about all things American.

The FBI and the state of New Jersey continue to pledge a $2 million reward for Chesimard's return to prison for her conviction in the murder of New Jersey Trooper Werner Foerster in 1973 ... My connection to Foerster's murder by Chesimard and several accomplices runs the breadth of my career ... From the time of her escape from a New Jersey prison on Nov. 2, 1979, to my deeper investigative involvement in her flight from justice while assigned to the FBI's Joint Terrorism Task Force in the mid-'80s and into my current role as colonel and superintendent, the New Jersey State Police and I have never lost the determination to see her returned to prison.

149

Fuentes also asks that U.S. travelers to Cuba visit the New Jersey State Police website for updated photos and bios of the terrorists living there, and, if seen, to contact the U.S. Embassy in Havana.

On April 30, 2015, H.R.2189—the "Walter Patterson and Werner Foerster Justice and Extradition Act," authored by Rep. Christopher Smith (Rep., NJ) with three cosponsors, was introduced. It would require the president to submit an annual report to Congress regarding U.S. efforts to obtain extradition of fugitives from U.S. justice. One of the proposed findings of the bill states, "The refusal of Cuba to extradite or otherwise render JoAnne Chesimard, an escaped convict who fled to Cuba after killing Werner Foerster, New Jersey State Trooper, is a deplorable example of a failure to extradite or otherwise render, and has caused ongoing suffering and stress to Mr. Foerster's surviving family and friends." The bill was referred to the House Committee on Foreign Affairs, which has not taken any action.

With the shift in relations between the United States and Cuba, there has been a renewed call for Cuba to extradite the woman U.S. law enforcement officials call a cop-killer and a terrorist; while at the same time, the woman who has become a folk hero in the eyes of supporters and black Americans believing her to be innocent.

Even the act of naming her reveals the depth of the schism. Law enforcement continues to call her JoAnne Chesimard. Her supporters know her by her chosen name, Assata Shakur. To law enforcement, JoAnne Chesimard is the killer convicted in the execution-style slaying of New Jersey State Trooper Werner Foerster in 1973. She is the Black Liberation Army leader busted out of prison by her comrades two years into a life sentence, a domestic terrorist implicated in a string of crimes and a key part of an organization that waged war on police.

To her supporters, Assata Shakur has been persecuted by the same corrupt and racist justice system that they say persecuted Michael Brown, the unarmed black teen killed in Ferguson, Missouri, in 2014, and Eric Garner, the Staten Island father of six who died from a chokehold that same year. During the protests in Ferguson,

Missouri, her name became a rallying cry. She has long been a revolutionary symbol, a radical black female often described as "the ultimate fugitive from injustice."

Others are calling for her to be pardoned. Change.org started a campaign to collect 100,000 signatures to deliver to the White House and to Governor Chris Christie. As of three years ago, there were still 6,670 signatures needed to reach 10,000. "There is much more to the issue than her deserving a pardon. Even if she were pardoned, she would not be safe here," Zayid Muhammad, chairman of the New Jersey Black Panther Party, told *The Final Call*.

The United States and Cuba have an extradition treaty dating back to 1905, and murder is one of the provisions that allows for extradition. But, Douglas McNabb, an international criminal lawyer specializing in extradition law, says: "Like many treaties between countries, there is also a provision that makes an exception for political offenses. And that language says not only that Cuba may not return those to whom it has granted political asylum, but that it cannot from the legal standpoint. That's the law. From a policy standpoint, states can do what they want and if Cuba wants to send her back, Cuba can do that, but I don't think that will happen."

Last year during an interview on "Democracy Now!" Lennox Hinds, long-time lawyer of Assata Shakur and member of the National Lawyers Guild, discussed Shakur's political asylum in Cuba:

The Cuban government granted Assata Shakur political asylum based on a firm grounding in international law, namely the Refugee Convention. There are precedents for U.S.-friendly nations that have refused to extradite American fugitives who have fled the U.S.; (such as), if an individual has a well-grounded fear that if they return to the country from which they left, they would either be persecuted or prosecuted based upon their political beliefs or/and their race or religion.

He further explained that in the 1970s, Black Panthers hijacked planes and went to France. France—an American ally which has signed international extradition treaties with the U.S.—conducted its own investigation and concluded the Panthers would be subject to racial and political oppression if they were returned to the States. As a result, France refused to extradite the Panthers.

Abdul Akbar Muhammad, International Representative of the Nation of Islam who travels to Cuba frequently, said: "I don't believe Cuba will extradite her … I don't believe they will extradite her because they are a principled country. We don't know all of the circumstances of her arrest and trial. Everything has not been brought to light and we see how Blacks are treated in the criminal justice system … Unless they plan on reopening the case and reexamining what happened, many people will be upset with bringing her back. If Cuba finds itself in a compromised position there are many other countries she would be welcomed in like Zimbabwe, South Africa and Ghana. They understand the struggles our people have been through. She could even go to Venezuela."

Despite the U.S. government pressing the issue, Cuban officials have repeatedly denied that extradition is negotiable. When asked if Cuba would send Shakur back, Gustavo Machin, the Deputy Director for American Affairs at the Cuban Ministry of Foreign Affairs, said, "It is off the table." The Cuban foreign ministry's head of North American affairs, Josefina Vidal, said Cuba would not return Shakur and that there is "no extradition treaty between Cuba and the U.S." If extradition ever becomes an option, there is the possibility that Cuba would request that the U.S. return Lois Posada Carriles, who was convicted for bombing a Cuban airliner in 1976 that killed 73 people, and was arrested in Panama for an attempting to assassinate Fidel Castro. Carriles is currently in asylum in the U.S, living out his life in Miami.

As recently as June 2016, according to a federal law-enforcement official as reported by NBC, there were discussions between the two countries that would bring about an exchange of Assata Shakur for Ana Montes, formerly a senior analyst for Cuban affairs with the U.S. Defense Intelligence Agency. On Sept. 21, 2001, Montes was arrested and charged with conspiracy to commit espionage for Cuba. She was sentenced to 25 years in prison and is scheduled to be released in 2023.

With everything considered, an extradition of Shakur seems unlikely for now. But, if the U.S. government continues to press the issue, Shakur's fate will move quickly from the periphery to the center of national media attention. Residents of Cuba as well as Assata supporters in the United States are saying that Assata, if she hasn't already fled, has another destination selected—another home that will welcome her as a political refugee—should the need arise. The probability of this happening increased when President Obama announced at the start of July that the U.S. would formally re-establish diplomatic ties with Cuba, and, therefore, would re-open embassies in both countries. "This is a historic step forward to normalize relations with the Cuban government and the people; to begin a new chapter with our neighbors in the Americas," said the POTUS.

In a July 2015 article written by Joshua Adams for *Ebony*, the effect of Shakur's extradition is examined:

The reactions to an unlikely, but still possible Shakur extradition would catapult #BlackLivesMatter to a larger international stage. Global protest movements for (alleged or proven) victims of political persecutions have happened before, such as the "Free Angela Davis and All Political Prisoners" campaign in the 70s and the movement to free Nelson Mandela in apartheid South Africa in the 80s. It is reasonable to surmise that returning Shakur to U.S. custody would spark an international protest of the same magnitude ....

There have been an estimated 1,500 police-related homicide victims since January of 2014. These killings, along with the non-indictments of the majority of the officers involved, has fueled a generation of activists to take #BlackLivesMatter from social media to the streets. Regardless of whether one asserts Shakur's guilt or innocence, she may be the most dramatic example in mainstream consciousness of a violent encounter between a White police officer and an unarmed black person that defied the conventional outcome.

... The extradition of a black activist "cop-killer" to a U.S. prison in an era of cops killing Blacks with impunity would be a spark on the powder keg ....

Shakur's extradition may further improve the fifty-year tumultuous relationship between the two governments; but it could also deepen racial divides within our country about what constitutes justice for all. Fidel Castro turned 90 in August; Raúl is only five years younger. At some point in the not-too-distant future, it will be determined whether or not this new relationship between the United States and Cuba can survive without a living Castro.

In April 2016, Cuba held its seventh Communist Party Congress in Havana announcing the results of its internal elections. President Raúl Castro will serve a second term as head of Cuba's Communist Party as the island's aging leaders see out a final period in power, amid economic reform and detente with the United States. The Communist Party wants to avoid any chaotic shake-up within its ranks as it wrestles with economic change and a transition from the generation of leaders who fought in the 1959 revolution.

Speaking at the closure of a four-day party congress, Raúl Castro, 85, said it would be the last one headed by the current party leaders, signaling that they would step aside sometime before the next such meeting in five years. "This seventh congress will be the last one led by the historic generation," Castro said, at the closing ceremony where delegates gave his elder brother, former president and revolutionary leader Fidel Castro, a roaring ovation. Fidel, the father of the Cuban revolution, died November 25, 2016.

As old doors close and new doors open, now, 43 years later at the age of 69, Assata Shakur continues to stand up for what she believes, for the black struggle, and let her voice be heard as that 20th century escaped slave, just as she did all those years ago. Perhaps the best description of how she defines herself today—of where she finds herself in relation to the world—is to revisit "Assante Sana" which Shakur wrote on her 60th birthday:

I realized that I was connected to Africa. I wasn't just a Colored girl. I was part of a whole world that wanted a better life. I'm part of a majority and not a minority. My life has been a life of growth. If you're not growing, you're not going to understand real love. If you're not reaching out to help others, then you're shrinking. My life has been active. I'm not a spectator.

We can't afford to be spectators while our lives deteriorate. We have to truly love our people and work to make that love stronger.

೮ ೮೮

Bibliography

Books

Browder, Laura. *Her Best Shot: Women and Guns in America.* Chapel Hill, North Carolina: UNC Press, 2009.

Camisa, Harry. Inside Out: Fifty Years behind the Walls of New Jersey's Trenton State Prison. Adelphia, New Jersey: Windsor Press and Publishing, 2003.

Cleaver, Kathleen and Katsiaficas, George. *Liberation, Imagination, and the Black Panther Party: A New Look at the Panthers and their Legacy.* New York, New York: Routledge, 2001.

Castellucci, John. *The Big Dance.* New York City, New York: Dodd Mead, 1986.

Churchill, Ward and James Vander Wall. *The Cointelpro Papers: documents from the FBI's secret wars against dissent in the United States.* Brooklyn, New York: South End Press, 2002.

Daley, Robert. *Target Blue.* New York City, New York: Dell Publishing, 1974.

James, Joy. Imprisoned Intellectuals: America's Political Prisoners Write on Life, Liberation, and Rebellion. Lanham, Maryland: Rowman & Littlefield, 2003.

Kunstler, William Moses. *My Life as a Radical Lawyer*. Secaucus, New Jersey: Birch Lane Press, 1994.

O'Reilly, Kenneth. *Racial Matters: The FBI's Secret File on Black America, 1960-1972*. New York City, New York: Collier Macmillan, 1972.

O'Rourke, John. *Jersey Troopers*. Gloucestershire, England: The History Press, 2010.

Perkins, Margo. *Autobiography as Activism: Three Black Women of the Sixties*. Jackson, Mississippi: University Press of Mississippi, 2000.

Rodriguez, Dylan. Forced Passages: Imprisoned Radical Intellectuals and the U.S. Prison Regime. Duluth, Minnesota: University of Minnesota Press, 2006.

Shakur, Assata. *Assata: An Autobiography*. Chicago, Illinois: Lawrence Hill Books, 2001.

Tomlinson, Gerald. *Murdered in Jersey*. New Brunswick, New Jersey: Rutgers University Press, 1994.

Van DeBurg, William. *New Day in Babylon: The Black Power Movement and American Culture*. Chicago, Illinois: University of Chicago Press, 1992.

Williams, Evelyn. Inadmissible Evidence: The Story of the African-American Trial Lawyer Who Defended the Black Liberation Army. Brooklyn, New York: Lawrence Hill Books, 2000.

Newspapers and Periodicals

Brath, Elombe. "N.J. Bloodhounds on Assata's Trail," *NY Daily Challenge*, March 13–15, 1998.

Daly, Michael. "The Msgr. & the Militant," *New York Daily News,* December 13, 2006.

Hanley, Robert. "Miss Chesimard Flees Jersey Prison, Helped By 3 Armed 'Visitors'," *The New York Times,* November 3, 1979.

Hinds, Lennox. "The injustice of the trial," *Covert Action Quarterly,* October 26, 1998.

_____ "The U.N. Petition," *Covert Action Quarterly*, October 26, 1998.

Jones, Robert A. "2 Die in Shootout; Militant Seized," *Los Angeles Times,* May 3, 1973.

Kaufman, Michael T. "Seized Woman Called Black Militants' Soul," *The New York Times,* May 3, 1973.

Kirsta, Alix. "A black and white case – Investigation – Joanne Chesimard," *The Times,* May 29, 1999.

Lichtenstein, Grace. "New Outbursts Mark Chesimard Trial," *The New York Times,* June 12, 1973.

Lubasch, Arnold H. "A Brink's Witness Testifies on the Chesimard Escape," *The New York Times,* May 4, 1983.

McFadden, Robert D. "Warrant Issued in Police Slaying," *The New York Times,* February 19, 1972.

Mueller, Robert S. III. "Wanted by the FBI – Fugitive – Joanne Deborah Chesimard," Federal Bureau of Investigation.

Obejas, Achy. "Why Cuba will never send Assata Shakur to the U.S.," *Chicago Tribune,* December 29, 2014.

Palmeri, Tara. "Cubans eye $2M reward for ratting out cop-killer," New York Post, December 27, 2014.

Sullivan, Joseph F. "Panther, Trooper Slain in Shoot-Out," *The New York Times,* May 3, 1973.

_____ "Chesimard Attorney Acts to Call Kelley; Wants FBI Director and Others to Testify on Program Aimed at Harassing Activists," *The New York Times,* February 24, 1977.

_____ "Chesimard Jury Asks Clarification of Assault Charges," *The New York Times,* March 25, 1977.

_____ "Assault Charges Add 26 Years to Mrs. Chesimard's Life Term," *The New York Times*, April 26, 1977.

Taylor, Mark Lewis. "Soapbox; Flight from Justice," *The New York Times,* January 17, 1999.

Waggoner, Walter H. "Woman Shot in Struggle with her Alleged Victim," *The New York Times,* April 7, 1971.

_____ "Joanne Chesimard Convicted in Killing of Jersey Trooper," *The New York Times,* March 26, 1977.

_____ "Jury in Chesimard Murder Trial Listens to State Police Radio Tapes," *The New York Times,* February 14, 1977.

"A Suspect in Panther's Death Here Is Slain by FBI in South," *The New York Times,* January 1, 1972.

"9 Black Liberation Suspects Indicted," *Los Angeles Times,* August 23, 1973.

"Black Militant Transferred," *The New York Times*, June 5, 1973.

"Miss Chesimard Transferred," *The New York Times,* May 15, 1973.

Internet

Almeida, Juan Juan. "Cuba: The Pitfalls of Extradition," www.14ymedio.com, April 23, 2015.

Chomsky, Noam. "Domestic Terrorism: Notes on the State System of Oppression," *New Political Science,* Volume 21, Number 3, September 1999.

Coleman, Kate. "Souled Out: Eldridge Cleaver Admits He Ambushed Those Cops," *New West*, May 19, 1980.

Erlich, Reese, October 1, 2015, www.commondreams.org.

Hanley, Robert. "Witness Calls Brinks' Killings Justified," *The New York Times,* September 13, 1983, http://www.nytimes.com/1983/09/13/nyregion/witness-calls-brink-s-killings-justified.html.

Harris, Paul. "FBI makes Joanne Chesimard the first woman to appear on most-wanted list," *The Guardian*, May 3, 2013.

Kupendua, Marpessa. "Sundiatta Acoli," *Revolutionary Worker,* No. 94, January 28, 1998.

Nisa, Islam Muhammad. "Movement grows to pardon freedom fighter Assata Shakur," *Final Call*, December 24, 2014, www.finalcall.com/artman/publish/National.../article_102017.shtml.

Porter, David. "Assata Shakur becomes first woman named to FBI's 'most wanted terrorists' list," *the Grio,* May 2, 2013.

Robbins, Tom. "Rebel with a Cause: Brooklyn Priest Father John Powis," June 10, 2009.

http://www.villagevoice.com/news/rebel-with-a-cause-brooklyn-priest-father-john-powis-6394303.

Spencer, Robyn. "Shakur, Assata (Chesimard, Joanne Deborah Bryon)," *Encyclopedia of African-American Culture and History*, 2006. http://www.encyclopedia.com.

Williams, Evelyn A. "Statement of Facts in the New Jersey trial of Assata Shakur," *The Talking Drum Collective*, June 25, 2005.

Wolf, Paul. "COINTELPRO: The Untold American Story," Presented to the U.N. High Commissioner for Human Rights Mary Robinson at the World Conference against Racism.

Woodruff, Barbara. "Joanne Chesimard, Convicted Murderer and Fugitive, named to FBI Most Wanted Terrorists List with $1 Million FBI Reward Offered for Information Leading to her Capture and Return," FBI Newark, May 3, 2013.

www.finalcall.com/artman/publish/National...2/article_8682.shtml.

http://www.njsp.org/wanted/chesimard.shtml.

https://www.fbi.gov/?came_from=https%3A//www.fbi.gov/wanted/dt/joanne-deborah-chesimard.

https://www.fbi.gov/news/stories/2013/may/joanne-chesimard-first-woman-named-most-wanted-

terrorists-list/joanne-chesimard-first-woman-named-to-most-wanted-terrorists-list.

http://thirdworldtraveler.com/FBI/COINTELPRO_Untold_Story.html, September 1, 2001.

www.eyesoftherainbow.com.

http://assataspeaks.net/index.htm.

http://www.njlawman.com/feature%20pieces/joanne%20chesimard.htm.

http://www.hartford-hwp.com/archives/45a/101.html.

https://en.wikipedia.org/wiki/Assata_Shakur.

http://www.blackpast.org/aah/freeman-beach-seabreeze-wilmington-north-carolina-ca-1885

http://www.myreporter.com/?p=1565

https://www.ourstate.com/oceanside-divide/#sthash.m0laHGbc.dpuf

https://natashabowens.wordpress.com/tag/freeman/

http://www.imdb.com/title/tt0107787/

http://marilynbuck.com/PP_status_international_law.html

http://www.nytimes.com/2007/05/12/world/americas/12cuba.html?ex
=1336622400&en=fa85c17a2e9e871f&ei=5088&partner=rssnyt&em
c=rss&_r=0

http://www.assatashakur.org/thecontinuityofstruggle.pdf

৪০ ෦ੲ

to my daughter kakuya
by assata shakur

i have shabby dreams for you
of some vague freedom
i have never known.
Baby
i don't want you hungry or thirsty
or out in the cold.
and i don't want the frost
to kill your fruit
before it ripens.

i can see a sunny place-
Life exploding green.
i can see your bright, bronze skin at ease with all the flowers
and the centipedes.

i can hear laughter,
not grown from ridicule
And words not prompted
by ego or greed or jealousy.

i see a world where hatred
has been replaced by love.
and ME replaced by WE

And I can see a world replaced
where you,
building and exploring,
strong and fulfilled,
will understand.
And go beyond
my little shabby dreams

ೞ ೞ   ೞ ೞ   ೞ ೞ

Index

Barbara Casey

ଓ ଔ   ଓ ଔ